Advance Praise for
Unschooling Critical Pedagogy, Unfixing Schools

"Testing, grading, tracking: the machinery of 'fixing' education. But what of the alternative? When critique becomes dogma, and that which once melted into air has regained its solidity, this book is just the solvent we need. Timely and incisive, it dares to challenge the shortcomings of the many on the educational left whose answers to the testing problems of our day have become ossified or neutralised by attrition and compromise. An alertness to the working of neoliberal ideology informs John E. Petrovic's perspective, cast uncompromisingly through the lens of Marxist analysis. It is to his credit that Petrovic revives the spirit of much maligned writers such as Althusser and Illich whose idiosyncratic emergence at a particular historical moment should not be seen to restrict their application now to the fixity of schooling for neoliberalism, and in so doing to propose unschooling (in school!) beyond the fetishisation of grades in their commodity form."
—Simon Boxley, *University of Winchester, United Kingdom*

"This is a very interesting and timely contribution to the discussions in the field of education. With the recent worldwide rise of extremism, both of the left and right, this book provides a well-balanced and thought-provoking discussion on the problems of, and need to (un)fix schools. There is a longstanding tradition of both liberal and conservative groups seeking to fix education and thereby applying their too often temporary solution. However, as the author suggests, it is our urge to try to control and fix education that might be the very problem with education; thus education needs to be *unfixed*. In addition, it also makes credible reference to some stimulating philosophical figures, such as Louis Pierre Althusser, and this adds strongly to the appeal of the volume. The format and general style make it very suitable for both students as well as academics."
—Alex Guilherme, *Pontifical Catholic University of Rio Grande do Sul, Brazil*

"John E. Petrovic's *Unschooling Critical Pedagogy, Unfixing Schools* provides provocative critiques of both liberal and progressive programs of school reform. Providing sharp critiques of mainstream and alternative attempts to transform schools, Petrovic accuses these efforts of trying to 'fix' the problem of schools as leaving the institutions intact. He instead suggests ways of 'unfixing schools' that will make schooling more open to their communities and making learning a more collaborative project that takes a multiplicity of forms to make schools more flexible and democratic while promoting freedom, criticality, conviviality, cooperation, and community. Petrovic's provocative analysis requires us to rethink schooling, critical pedagogy, and our own processes of teaching and learning."
—Douglas Kellner, *George F. Kneller Philosophy of Education Chair, UCLA*

Unschooling Critical Pedagogy, Unfixing Schools

This book is part of the Peter Lang Education list.
Every volume is peer reviewed and meets
the highest quality standards for content and production.

PETER LANG
New York • Bern • Berlin
Brussels • Vienna • Oxford • Warsaw

John E. Petrovic

Unschooling Critical Pedagogy, Unfixing Schools

PETER LANG
New York • Bern • Berlin
Brussels • Vienna • Oxford • Warsaw

Library of Congress Cataloging-in-Publication Data
Names: Petrovic, John E., author.
Title: Unschooling critical pedagogy, unfixing schools / John E. Petrovic.
Description: New York: Peter Lang, 2019.
Includes bibliographical references and index.
Identifiers: LCCN 2018047547 | ISBN 978-1-4331-6185-8 (hardcover: alk. paper)
ISBN 978-1-4331-6181-0 (paperback: alk. paper) | ISBN 978-1-4331-6182-7 (ebook pdf)
ISBN 978-1-4331-6183-4 (epub) | ISBN 978-1-4331-6184-1 (mobi)
Subjects: LCSH: Critical pedagogy.
Capitalism and education.
Educational change.
Philosophy, Marxist.
Dialectical materialism.
Classification: LCC LC196 .P49 2019 | DDC 370—dc23
LC record available at https://lccn.loc.gov/2018047547
DOI 10.3726/b14805

Bibliographic information published by **Die Deutsche Nationalbibliothek**.
Die Deutsche Nationalbibliothek lists this publication in the "Deutsche Nationalbibliografie"; detailed bibliographic data are available on the Internet at http://dnb.d-nb.de/.

© 2019 Peter Lang Publishing, Inc., New York
29 Broadway, 18th floor, New York, NY 10006
www.peterlang.com

All rights reserved.
Reprint or reproduction, even partially, in all forms such as microfilm, xerography, microfiche, microcard, and offset strictly prohibited.

TABLE OF CONTENTS

Acknowledgments	vii
Introduction: Unschooling Critical Pedagogy and Unfixing Education	1
Chapter 1. Fixing Education	15
Chapter 2. Unfixing Education with Critical Pedagogy	35
Chapter 3. Critical Pedagogy within an Ideological State Apparatus	59
Chapter 4. Unschooling Against the Ideological State Apparatus	85
Chapter 5. Unschooling in and out of Schools	109
Chapter 6. Authenticity, Identity Politics, and Critical Pedagogy	135
References	153
Index	165

ACKNOWLEDGMENTS

This book builds on several previous works, which are reproduced to varying degrees. I am grateful to Sage, Taylor & Francis, and Springer Publishing for permission to reuse those articles in this way. Specifically, Chapter 3 adds to Petrovic and Kuntz (2018) and Kuntz and Petrovic (2018). Chapter 4 owes to Petrovic and Rolstad (2017). Chapter 5 borrows again from Kuntz and Petrovic (2018).

In addition to acknowledging our previous work together, I need to thank Aaron Kuntz for our many conversations that went toward the development of this larger project. His insights into connecting, as an example, Marx and Althusser to the new materialism that is the thrust of his current work were invaluable.

I am also grateful to Cindy Jones who dutifully and carefully proofread each chapter. She also took the lead in the tedium of putting together the index.

In the end, I must dedicate this project to my children, Sophie and Lucas, who would have liked nothing more than the permission to resist more forcefully than they did the process of being schooled.

INTRODUCTION: UNSCHOOLING CRITICAL PEDAGOGY AND UNFIXING EDUCATION

> Education either functions as an instrument which is used to facilitate integration of the younger generation into the logic of the present system and bring about conformity or it becomes the practice of freedom, the means by which men and women deal critically and creatively with reality and discover how to participate in the transformation of their world.—Freire, *Pedagogy of the Oppressed*

Often, in mainstream and scholarly publications alike, one encounters proclamations of the need to fix education. Though authors, politicians, and policy analysts may begin from radically different political and philosophical positions, they often similarly point to a broken educational system. For some, schooling does not do enough to maintain an economically productive citizenry, failing to promote students with the technical skills needed to meet the needs of the world order. For others, contemporary educational systems serve only to reinscribe dangerous neoliberal models, failing to instill a critical sensibility in students and constraining opportunities for social change. Still others perhaps point to the inherent dangers within the school walls themselves—the means by which students are made more vulnerable to a massifying education when they walk through the schoolhouse door.[1]

In other words, both conservative and critical pedagogues (and others in between) strive to reform an institutional system that, through its very formation, enacts a limiting effect on student potential. That said, let me not beat around the bush and note that I begin from the premise that, even some eighty years on, it is the case that Counts' (1932) claim that "almost everywhere [the existing school] is in the grip of conservative forces" continues to describe the manufactured status quo. This is, of course, not an uncontested assertion, as exemplified by E. D. Hirsch's *The Schools We Need*. Yet interestingly, both critical and conservative approaches to schooling proclaim rather similar goals: Both Counts earlier and Hirsch now seek a more democratic, equal, and fair social order, albeit from radically different foundations and, ultimately, it must be said, radically different visions of "democracy." Beyond the similarity of such foundations (at least rhetorically), these groups share a fundamental flaw in their idealist vision of "just" schooling. Though conservatives and criticalists perhaps espouse different values and social assumptions as rationale for reforming schools, they both seek to "fix" schools. This volume walks through the theoretical and philosophical foundations of *un*fixing schools, ending with some recommendations as to how to engage such a project.

I will argue that in the move to fix, criticalists and conservatives either deny or misread the material dimension of schooling, thereby unnecessarily limiting possibilities for human flourishing within educational environments. On the one hand, criticalists seem to have lost the thread of how to engage the problem practically. This, too, requires analytical reengagement—as I will point out in Chapter 2. On the other hand, conservatives fail or refuse to engage the problem analytically, at least from analytic frames that promote the basic Liberal ideals they claim to hold. Their perennial alarm about "progressive" or "liberal" schools suggests that they would like to reclaim traditional formations of social order through "innovative" pedagogical practices aimed at producing a docile and individual-centric citizenry. However, as I will argue, the contemporary conservative agenda simply accelerates and amplifies the economic values and rationale that have driven principles of schooling for decades. Thus, through their denial of the material dimension of schools, conservatives exacerbate the reproduction of existing social relations, embracing a deep and problematic indoctrination into a free market, corporate ideology.

Hirsch (1996), for example, argues that naturalistic principles that undergird child-centered education are fundamentally flawed and freedom should be replaced with the promotion of grade level readiness driven by national standards with particularly defined outcomes and monitoring through specific accountability arrangements to include testing, external and enforceable incentives, and sanctions (pp. 227–229). In such conservative thinking, denying freedom somehow promotes a more freely developed and sustainable individual. Such educational futurism—educating students for future needs of society as opposed to children's own present interests and needs—is highly problematic by its own goals. For it is an education of conformity, education for the collective, not the individual. In this way, Hirsch, and conservatives generally, performs a contemporary brand of Orwellian double-speak.

On the other hand, according to Counts, critically inclined progressives rightly "focused attention squarely upon the child, recognized the fundamental importance of the interest of the learner, defended the thesis that activity lies at the root of all true education, conceived learning in terms of life situations and growth of character, and have championed the rights of the child as free personality" (pp. 5–6). Nevertheless, progressive education lacked critical direction for Counts and he, like Hirsch, criticized progressive education for its "extreme freedom" (p. 10), a critique that questioned how individually focused freedoms might give rise to the collective-spirit necessary for social justice work. I have noted elsewhere (Petrovic, 1998) that Hirsch is simply wrong in the way that he characterizes the notion of freedom as employed by democratic progressives (such as John Dewey, Hirsch's primary target in this vein). Notice, however, that Counts provides a very different rationale in his critique of progressive freedom. For Counts, progressive education became a form of hyperindividuality (and, hence, conservative) and did not emphasize enough the need to educate for conviviality, to educate toward living within a collective society. Unlike conservative education—which, in fact, does not even recognize the collectivity problem—the critique from Counts' perspective is in regard to a lack of balance.

Drawing on critical theory, contemporary criticalists, of course, have sought to provide such balance through a focus on social justice. Even so, freedom or the lack thereof must remain a concern within contemporary schools. Essentially, the approaches of conservative schooling and critical pedagogy mis-present the material context of schooling to such an extent that their respective philosophical approaches to education become contradictory, failing the promises for social change. As I have tried to intimate, this "failing" is reasonably straightforward in regard to conservatives but requires a more complicated explanation vis-à-vis criticalists.

As such, through this book, I consider the material dimensions of schooling as constitutive of the possibilities inherent in "fixing" education. In education, the infinite loop of invoking the necessity of change in the abstracted, amaterialist language of reform often leads to feeling overwhelmed by the impact of social diagnosis—that radical changes to education can never outpace the propensity for schooling to reinscribe contemporary ideology. "Fixing" education remains bound to the very logic formations that rendered schooling a recognizable problem. Like the many critics who come before me, I begin with an assumption that contemporary formations of education do not produce an engaged and deliberative democracy. At the same time, I remain concerned that the very corrective measures intended to improve education reinscribe those values, practices, and common sense that I believe got us in to this mess from the beginning. Thus it is that critics of education—whether conservative, liberal, or progressive in espoused politics—do a disservice to the radical possibilities of education: they fix it to death.

In order to begin to address this problem, I start by mapping out the notion of "fixing education" as a normative exercise in containing the liberatory potential of human flourishing. Here, educational reform, though intended to invoke change, actively reconstitutes an antimaterial sensibility with significant consequences for democracy. The notion of "fixing" is multiple and I submit that several meanings are in play when it comes to education. In addition to defining *to fix* as "to mend or repair," the *Oxford English Dictionary* notes the verb as an action against movement: "to make stable"; "to secure from change"; "to deprive of volatility or fluidity"; "to make fast or permanent." More colloquially, one might understand a conspiratorial sense of the term: "the fix is in." Beyond mere wordplay, I understand contemporary, conservative formations of schooling to draw upon a collusion of all three forms of this term: politicians and citizens alike proclaim a need to fix education, most often through aligning schooling with the processes and practices of some imagined past (thereby avoiding any possibility for a radical, unforeseen, or unanticipated future). In this way, conservative proponents of educational reform draw from key components of what Michael Apple (2006) has termed *conservative modernization*—acting on its components as though they are a matter-of-course.[2] There is thus a violence to such fixity; indeed, a degree of death.

I take up this particular manifestation of "fixing" in the first chapter. I provide an overview of what I see as the contemporary state of affairs dominated by conservative modernization. Conservative modernization is a general movement driven by several interrelated and sometimes coordinated submovements including conservativism, neoconservativism, and authoritarian populism. This alliance has exerted increasing influence over educational policy and reform. While I will note the ways in which each of these movements is working to reform education, I will emphasize the role of what I consider the dominant movement: neoliberalism.

I argue that deprivation of fluidity (stasis) is the repair sought by conservative modernization. The values and practices of this enhanced conservatism assert narrowly select possibilities for learning while confining others. This process constructs students in problematic ways and examples abound within education: test scores stand in for student identity, linked together to grant a determination for what a student *is* (a good student, a high/low-achieving student, etc.); teachers are applauded or reprimanded for the degree to which their students statistically improve[3]; schools are deemed "successful" or "failing" based on the historical trajectory of student outcome measures; the US educational system is shown to be "falling behind" other countries (namely Japan and Germany) in science and math, etc. What binds these examples is an adherence to a normative neoliberal logic that determines contemporary identities based on a static presentation of historical (statistical) outcomes.

This collapse of the present with the past fixes identities and practices, binding them to specifically recognized and historically produced data points. As a consequence, future possibility—what one might be, what one has yet to become—is similarly bound, fixed by the comparative logic of measurement and accountability reflected in the statistic, the data points that stand in for the child. In this sense, those processes and practices that exist outside or in excess of the neoliberal order are rendered illegitimate and/or disciplined into fixed relation with those neoliberal values that mark the status quo; they are normalized. Importantly, this process of normalization manifests in the very material conditions/circumstances in which we are immersed.

Having established such normative means for fixing education through capturing its possibility, "the fix is in" to maintain a reformulated inequitable status quo required of neoliberal social formations. Here schooling becomes a static space of bureaucracy. Thus, the discussion in this chapter will make clear that conservative modernization is a movement to nowhere, much like a hubcap that continues to spin long after the tire has stopped. In other words, conservative modernization is, in the main, a reinscription of dominant societal forces, of the status quo. It reinvokes the governing rationale which makes it a circular system.

Such stasis requires recognizing contemporary education as a form of necrophilia, "fixing" education in ways that make static otherwise naturally fluid processes-of-living and what it means to learn. Educational fixity extends from—and furthers—a conservatively modern project that situates "legitimate" workers as technicians, skilled at operating the machinery of capitalism, yet never questioning the procedures of which they are a part (and through which they are known or interpellated). I articulate the material realities of the move within the conservative restoration to fix. Here, I recognize the many ways in which normative practices and processes collude to produce socially sustained and individually encountered effects of anxiety and insecurity that, in turn, give a degree of manufactured urgency to the project of fixing institutions such as education.

Indeed, as Chomsky (2016) observes, "Policy is designed to create insecurity." In neoliberal economics, policy makers seek to create "greater worker insecurity," as Alan Greenspan, former Chair of the Federal Reserve in the United States, recommended. In education policy, anxiety is created through an emphasis on economic productivity such that students are increasingly funneled into studies that have been determined to best serve the needs of the economy. Measurement and accountability become hallmarks to determine the potentially most productive students toward these narrow ends. In other words, education must be fixed to reflect and reinscribe the principles and values of conservative modernization. Just as neoliberalism manufactures worker insecurity to do this on a broad scale, we must also seek, as the Ontario Minister of Education recommended in a leaked memo (Pinto, 2012), "invent a crisis" in education. This is hardly surprising self-preservation. As Freire (1973) observed of the elite, "perceiving more clearly the threat involved in the awakening of popular consciousness, they organize. They bring forth a group of 'crisis theoreticians' … they create social assistance institutions and armies of social workers; and—in the name of supposedly threatened freedom—they repel the participation of the people" (p. 14).

Beyond the overt manifestation of neoliberal doctrine, "fixing" education most dangerously extends from subtle practices often overlooked due to their adherence to standardized logics of common sense. The problem here is, as Max Horkheimer (1972) observed, "the facts which our senses present to us are socially preformed" (p. 200). In this scenario, one attends to select social problems through remedies that extend from the governing rationality that made such problems visible in the first place. In this instance, only slight reforms to the effects of the status quo are possible, not radical changes beyond current practice. As Albert Einstein is alleged to have quipped, "We can't solve problems by using the same kind of thinking we used when we created them."

Thus, I explain conservative modernization not in terms of movement, but in terms of fixity. Indeed, this analysis will run throughout the first three chapters employing distinct conceptual tools. Given this, the question at the root of this project is how to escape the centrifugal force created by conservative modernization, how to create real movement, or, as I put it, how to "unfix" education. Critical pedagogy is, of course, an effort toward that end.

Toward the end of Chapter 1, I begin my own performance of movement toward unfixing. Here I review some of the basic tenets of Liberalism.[4] If "fixing" education is a dishonest and incessantly normative project inherently linked to the material realities of our contemporary time, a response to these processes must find its source of or motivation for reinvigoration somewhere, even or perhaps most effectively from within. For it is demonstrably clear that the centrifugal force of conservative modernization undermines the very ideals its proponents purport to defend. Some critical scholars might dismiss this either as antithetical to the otherwise overarching Marxian framing I want to claim or as the folly of employing "the master's tools" which, as Audrey Lorde (1984) famously declared, "will never dismantle the master's house" (p. 112).

First, I would argue that economic justice is a prerequisite to making basic tenets of Liberalism (such as autonomy and freedom, which are, in fact, worthy of defense) robust enough to fulfill their promise. Focusing on the most salient feature of inequality in contemporary capitalist societies also begins to inculcate a sense of (in)justice more broadly. Second, it is a mistake to abandon ideals fundamental to the sociopolitical context and the dominant discourse through which criticalists are most likely to gain a foothold. Thinking about these ideals differently, through a different lens, is not the same as "using the same kind of thinking," as Einstein demurred. Third, the basic tenets that I will discuss—namely, autonomy, freedom, and flourishing—are all part and parcel of the Marxist tradition. Conscientization for Freire and self-consciousness for Hegel are logically the search for autonomy. Simultaneously, this is the search for freedom. To wit, in *Philosophy of Right*, Hegel argues that man must take possession of himself by becoming conscious of himself as free. For Marx, freedom cannot obtain where inequality drives the capitalist mode of production and class division; such gross inequality of condition creates serfdom for the many. Such class division resultant from capitalist relations of production must be undone. For the alienation that derives from such relations imposes a lack of autonomy, self-realization, and flourishing. Thus it is important to remember the words that precede Lorde's (1984) famous declaration and that we learn "how to make common cause with those others identified as outside the structures in order to define and seek a world in which we can all flourish. It is learning how to take our differences and make them strengths" (p. 112).

Given that a Marxian approach further animates the possibility inherent in the principal tenets of Liberalism, Marx remains essential to both the ideal of Liberalism and critical pedagogy. In order to understand the necessity of Marx, I begin Chapter 2 with an overview of orthodox Marxism, including Marx's own notion of movement captured in his historical and dialectical materialism. I then trace the influence of Marx on critical theory, mainly through the work of leading members of the Frankfurt School, Max Horkheimer and Theodore Adorno. The discussion then turns, in logical succession, to the role of critical theory in critical pedagogy.

Here I briefly review the roots of critical pedagogy through Marxism and, subsequently, neo-Marxism in the form of critical theory as a means to promote social justice and flourishing against the reproductive role of schools as forces of neoliberalism and, ultimately, forms of governmentality. Ideally, critical pedagogy was not only an important move against neoliberalism initially, but also, more contemporarily, an important source of critique of uncritical liberalism, a liberalism that often manifests in schools as multiculturalism. This multiculturalism—while perhaps necessary—was (and remains) a fetishization, a form of shallow political correctness that, as such, served conservatism in a twofold way: exploited by the right as a "concession" that could simultaneously be attacked as political correctness that quite effectively drew a line of this-far-left and no further. Critical pedagogy, as a movement within the social justice movement, was important to pushing that line. Nevertheless, even as a particular outgrowth of Marxism, critical pedagogy has failed to take on the materialist challenge to institutions.

Therefore, the question I try to build toward is whether or not and/or to what extent the application of a Marxian frame addresses fixity. Certainly key notions within critical pedagogy, such as Freire's praxis and his critique of instrumental rationality in favor of emancipatory reason, create, to some extent, the movement I seek. Indeed, I continue to highlight and critique throughout this project, now from an explicitly Marxian perspective, examples of neoliberal influences on educational reform. On the one hand, I will argue that contemporary instantiations of critical pedagogy, even as they offer proper and useful critiques of normative education, have lost the necessary rootedness in orthodox Marxism. One effect of this has been the loss of the collective autonomy that Marxists like Freire emphasize. On the other hand, the movement within Marx, dialectical materialism, provides merely the illusion of autonomy which can only feed back into and enhance the forces of conservative modernization. This is a primary point at which critical pedagogy stalls. I will suggest that a problem here is an overreliance on "Hegelian" rationalism—even as it presents movement itself through the dialectic. This stems, in part, on thin conceptions and practice of Freire's problem-posing approach.

Stepping back, it seems that this particular problem also stems, in part, from the inherent problem of the fixed notion of ideology within Marxism. As such, the subject in Marxism is always already an object and, therefore, just as fixed as they would be in neoliberalism. The Marxist root of critical pedagogy is necessary but insufficient, as critical pedagogy fails to fully engage with the material dimensions of schooling. In so doing, critical pedagogy can cut off key possibilities for human flourishing within educational environments.

In Chapter 3, I attempt to remedy the failure of critical pedagogy to take on the reproductive materialism of schools by drawing on the work of Louis Althusser. Althusser maintains the necessary connection to Marx while providing the tools for a more robust interrogation of and movement away from conservative modernization and fixity. Thus, in this chapter, I provide an Althusserian take on ideology, an understanding of ideology as functioning in myriad ways in contrast to Marx's ideological singularity. Furthermore, as I point out in Chapter 2, Hegel is of greater help here than often suggested. For Hegel is as much a materialist as he is an idealist.

Essentially, schools, as institutional features of society, are part of the superstructure and, hence, the ideological material. As such, they function as ideological state apparatuses, reinscribing the existing social order. Under such understanding, I seek to relocate critical pedagogy outside its current, stagnated, schooled formulation—consisting of "bending the rules" to read dangerous books or telling kids that texts are biased social constructions of some privileged reality (Wink, 2005). In other words, I argue that critical pedagogy has no transformative potential absent an engaged materialist understanding. Otherwise, as its predecessor multicultural education, conventional critical pedagogy is a form of "managed care" (Garvey, 1996), operating self-contradictorily in pushing the limits within the bounds of traditional schools. In the end, the material conditions within schools, as ideological state apparatuses, simply overwhelm critical pedagogy. This is because it suffers from an insufficient theory of experience.

In schools, both teachers and students experience their own commodification through the standards and accountability (testing) regime that currently dominates the schooling experience.[5] This regime derives directly from corporate discourse with one of its key terms being "value added." Consider how value added is defined at *Investopedia*. For investors, the term "describes the enhancement a company gives its product or service before offering the product to customers." Thus, children become products and teachers capitalists in their development. Their approaches to learning and teaching, respectively, adapt accordingly. Interpellation at its finest.

The necessary critique of the movements within conservative modernization—now, from an Althusserian framing, cast as cultural invasion and imperialist nostalgia—continues through Chapter 3. Through this critique, I will argue that the move from Marx to Althusser provides insights into a much more active engagement with the material. This is because, as just suggested, Althusser understands ideology as being constructed and manifested in myriad ways, thus opening more points of engagement. In other words, Althusser moves us to engage differently with the dialectical. Indeed, from this lens, I necessarily transition away from the dialectical and rational synthesis to the multilectical and engagement with the ideological. Schools, in their very materiality, remain open spaces of liberating possibility. In this sense, educational spaces must not be interpreted simplistically as solely reproductive of the dominant social order but also as inevitably productive, making possible challenges to the contemporarily unjust social order even as they reaffirm the principal values and practices of the dominant neoliberal model. The materiality of schools always remains in excess of the normative logic that governs education.[6] In order to engage with this excessive potential, one must begin by mapping the space of education—identifying areas where schooling might be reanimated as a radical form of democratic engagement.

It is the work of critical pedagogues to identify points of intervention (e.g., ending competitive grading). Such points are what Simon Boxley (2017) identifies when he raises a crucial, practical question: "to what extent [I would add, 'and how'] can the conscious Marxist intervene in the ideological process early such as to at least offset the full force of ideological reproduction?" (p. 107). This, of course, has been an ongoing and yet unresolved question for critical pedagogues and, not surprisingly, Boxley does not lead us to some holy, Marxist, pedagogical grail here. For the "conscious Marxist," change—if it is not to come by revolution—is necessarily incremental, coming through subversive education and pedagogical sabotage of bourgeois, neoliberal education. Such sabotage is necessary to reveal the extent to which the consciousness of the oppressed is not really theirs but that of the oppressor, as Freire (1989) argues. This state of affairs comes about through the material conditions generated for and by capitalism.

Nevertheless, the Marxist must recognize that such incrementality, while hopeful, is simply insufficient to counteract the material conditions of schooling. Working within the ideological state apparatus of schools as they currently manifest in this way simply leaves the left to, in Tyack and Cuban's (1995) words, tinker toward utopia. Thus, the bigger question here is that if critical pedagogy cannot deal with Marx's singularity, and is left to simple tinkering, how can it deal sufficiently with the multifaceted ideological functioning revealed by Althusser? Indeed, from this perspective, the material conditions which become fixed for Marx are in constant motion for Althusser. Paradoxically, then, such motion of the material conditions within schools helps to reinscribe fixity by adding to the ideological centrifugal force of conservative modernization.

Given this, I turn, in Chapter 4, to a discussion of unschooling as a potentially more fruitful approach. Like Boxley, I continue to believe in the radical possibility that is education, an understanding that the social and material spaces afforded schooling make possible a vision for social justice and critical democracy. Despite their constricting effect on freedom and criticality, following Foucault (1984), I recognize that the material spaces of schooling are never simply static containers of oppression (as left and right leaning critics alike might find) but also exist as open working spaces that remain generative due to their inability to ever be fully defined. The unschooling movement blurs the line between formal institutions of education and educational practices, complicating definition and, thus, enhancing the creation of heterotopic spaces. It does so by engaging the materially *public* spaces of schools.

To carry this point, I link more contemporary work in materialism back to the work of Jean Jacques Rousseau to review and add to a philosophy of unschooling. Building on Petrovic and Rolstad (2017), I draw on Althusser to align materialism with Rousseau's radical roots as an "unschooler." Situating education with the promotion of moral citizenship, what Rousseau provides that Althusser does not is a philosophy of education that corresponds to the social theory. Of course, the work of Paolo Freire necessarily factors into such a discussion but does not complete it. For Rousseau also offers us an element of human flourishing that is not found in either the neoliberal or criticalist tradition. In a sense, I am tracing the contemporary unschooling movement (and the work of notables such as A. S. Neill, Ivan Illich, and John Holt) back to the work of Rousseau, again, in order to "blur the line."

One way to do this is to reconnect schools to living as opposed to working. Toward this end, some unschoolers, such as A. S. Neill or Ivan Illich, argue that critical education did not go far enough. Contrary to both Hirsch and Counts, for example, for unschoolers more freedom and more child-centeredness are required. For too much learning and not enough play characterize the institution of schooling. To the extent that critical pedagogy is consumed within the material reality of schooling, I want to suggest that unschooling is a necessary corrective that broadens the public-ness of education. These are the spaces where fixity fails—possibility extends from unschooling schools, from unfixing the process of fixing education. It does so by providing (1) a sustained engagement with the philosophical assumptions of schools as institutions; (2) a democratic practice of learning and, ultimately, flourishing; and (3) a recognition of the promises inherent in a materialist framework. Nevertheless, given this third point, it is necessary to note that even as unschoolers recognize the material effects of the institution of schooling, they similarly misread material social realities *outside* of school.

Therefore, in Chapter 5, I argue that unschooling, while perhaps pointing to a way to overcome the limiting effects of critical pedagogy in school, does not provide a complete solution. Drawing on conceptualizations and descriptions of unschooling in the growing contemporary unschooling movement—as demonstrated by the proliferation of websites, books (often self-published by unschooling parents), and the Journal of Unschooling and Alternative Learning (founded in 2006)—I critique the unschooling frame for ignoring the material conditions and social relations that occur *outside* of schools and ask if current instantiations of unschooling can challenge the contemporary status quo. I draw on Althusser's dialectical approach to materialism as a productive means for engaging critical pedagogy and radicalize the unschooling movement. In other words, the limitations of both critical pedagogy and unschooling require a newly critical project that takes seriously the materialist realities of schooling in our contemporary times.

In order to create schools as heterotopias, more layers of meaning and more points of comparison and more mirrors of our experiences must be added. The lines must be more completely blurred. Thus, the specific goal of this project is to work through the educational orientations of critical schooling (as critical pedagogy) toward a philosophy and model of education that dwells in the possibility of the not-yet determined. I attempt to develop some potential for things to be other than they are (or currently envisioned to be). Having dismissed traditional/conservative schooling and having also argued that the critical pedagogy movement, as currently conceptualized, is incapable of promoting the kind of change that we still need, I offer a hybrid approach of *unschooling in school*. This necessarily comes in addition to received accounts of unschooling, models of which typically take place out of schools. Combined, these approaches provide the direction Counts sought by (1) recognizing the conservative reproductive power of schools as institutions and the limited extent to which such power can be successfully challenged, and (2) seeking to deal with the material dimension of the broader socioeconomic-political landscape—something that unschoolers did not do.

This multiple hybridity recognizes that the institution of organized schooling is necessary since it is within that space that pedagogy can be given direction. Schools *can be* sites of critical reflection: organized places wherein the obstacles and contradictions of dominant social relations can be revealed and deliberated within the system itself. Such contradictions open possibilities for reflection and, thus, intervention as we move forward in hopes for social justice. In other words, the material possibilities of public education remain a valuable entry point for the work of social justice. As such, this hybrid philosophy seeks to provide an answer to the following questions: What is the role of schooling vs. unschooling in the interpellation of the subject? What animates intervention beyond critical reflection? Answers to such questions ultimately point toward unschooling generally and unschooling in schools specifically. For, on the one hand, while critical reflection is necessary to autonomy, it is unschooling, by functioning outside the delimiting material conditions of the institution, that creates the persons as free subjects. Even so, and on the other hand, this must also occur in school through critical pedagogy such that the school itself serves as an entry point for social change that works to radicalize the very system of which it is a part.

The significance of this project begins with the recognition that institutional arrangements shape education and any attempts to fix or unfix it. Such arrangements can interpellate (Althusser, 2014) both teachers and students either as critical subjects or as docile objects. Historically, it has been the latter, occluding teachers' and students' subjection by the material conditions of myriad social institutions. Such are the consequences of an incessant desire to fix education which must, instead, be *unfixed*.

Notes

1. Massification is a term employed by Freire in reference to primary effects of schooling, which are to disengage students from reality, leading them to conform and accept uncritically that society simply is what it is. This is a notion to which I return in subsequent chapters.
2. In many ways, my argument here aligns with Peter Roberts' (2014) recognition that politicians in New Zealand crafted public policy with the assumption that globalization was a material reality, as though it is a concrete *thing*. Similarly, politicians assume the necessity of fixing schools in particular ways, as though neoliberal rationality was a pre-given reality unto itself.
3. At the time of this writing the state legislature in Alabama was considering the "Raise Act" that would essentially base teacher salaries primarily on student outcome measures. Teacher educational attainment (whether gaining an advanced degree or acquiring additional graduate coursework) would no longer be part of the equation.
4. I tend to capitalize Liberalism, especially when clearly speaking to the political theory as opposed to the political orientation, i.e., liberal vs conservative.
5. It may be important to note here that Freire supported many of the practices that I will cast as a problematically neoliberal, for example, traditional school grading systems (cf. Gibson, 2006).
6. Throughout this project I use terms such as *education*, *schooling*, and *school* with the recognition that they convey both material and discursive properties. This is, one cannot talk about *a school*, for example, absent the material contexts in which it is immersed or the discursive formations of educational policy and curriculum.

· 1 ·

FIXING EDUCATION

> In the Swedish case, we conclude that the implementation of neoliberal policies in education has resulted in increased inequality, segregation of vulnerable social groups, lower performance, market-oriented teachers and less democratic citizenship. Learning has become individualized, competitive and performance driven. Creativity and students' initiatives are marginalized and collective methods of learning are hardly functioning.—Symeonidis (2014, p. 35)

In this chapter, I set the motivation for this project which is, in large part, to challenge the conservatively modern ethos of the contemporary order. Toward this end, I present an understanding of various forces of conservative modernization and the ways that it manifests and functions within schools. To the extent that these forces dominate schools, manifesting through policy, curricula, and pedagogy, among other things, formal education certainly cannot "build a new social order" with radically democratic ends. Indeed, such forces will obviously function not to challenge but to reinscribe themselves. After all, conservativism conserves. While it may largely be a review for many readers of a text like this, it is nevertheless necessary to review understandings of conservative modernization and its effects on schools in order to lay a foundation for subsequent arguments.

Building on the different definitions of "fixing" addressed in the introduction, I argue that conservative modernization manifests simultaneously in three notions of fixing: as repair, as stasis, and as corruption or manipulation. As I noted, "fixing education" in these terms becomes a normative exercise in containing the liberatory potential of human flourishing. To the extent that the initial proclamations of the need to fix continue to manufacture crises and undermine a radically democratic future, there is not only violence but also a degree of death—in the form of necrophilia as I argue more thoroughly in Chapter 3—inherent in fixity. This death is revealed, in part, by the way that the policies and practices of educational reform, born of conservative modernization, employ, yet undermine, basic Liberal ideals that this congeries purports to defend. For my purposes, I will focus on freedom, autonomy, and flourishing. More than a rhetorical device, attempts to fix education are framed within historically Liberal ideals yet manifest within material contexts as enactments of conservatively modern principles and practices.

Conservative Modernization

Conservative modernization might usefully be understood as a "hegemonic bloc of social forces that collude to effect conservative changes in education" (Kuntz, Gildersleeve, Pasque, 2011, p. 489). This movement accelerates through the entangled relation of four groups, identified by Apple (2006) as *neoliberals, neoconservatives, authoritarian populists, and the new managerial middle class*. Through their relation, these groups manufacture select ways of thinking through mutually identified problems and practical solutions—together, they fix.

As a term often invoked in contemporary theorizations of education (though less often defined) *neoliberalism* exists as the transformation of social practices, identities, and values into economic equivalencies. Neoliberalism situates hyper-individualism, surveillance, and privatization as commonsensical values through which ostensibly positive social change (read: fixity) may occur. Given this, I should raise at the outset my tendency to switch back and forth from discussions of capitalism and neoliberalism. In a previous article (Petrovic & Kuntz, 2018), Aaron Kuntz and I understood neoliberalism generally as the current manifestation of capitalism, or, as Giroux notes, "the latest stage of *predatory* capitalism" (emphasis added, Interview with V. Harper, 2014, p. 1078). There are, of course, many forms of neoliberalism and attempts at a pure definition inevitably fail. Nevertheless, these forms share a number of characteristics including, among other things, economic Darwinism, ever-expanding material wealth and the concentration of that wealth in the hands of a few, and the promotion of consumption as citizenship (Giroux, 2014).

I understand that the conflation of capitalism and neoliberalism as well as this generalized understanding of neoliberalism (as opposed to neoliberalisms) might be problematic in a more historicized and orthodox reading, yet I do not think it detracts from my purposes here. This said, however, I do want to add to this general understanding that neoliberalism is qualitatively distinct from capitalism. As Azar (2015) notes, the authoritarianism of neoliberalism within the state "is present not only in its unquestioned defense of the interests of capital, but also in the way that it actively seeks to shape society to be more favorable to its goals" (p. 100). (In this way, the fixity of neoliberalism becomes corruption and/or manipulation.) This understanding of neoliberalism serves as an interpretive lens through which to view the other movements within conservative modernization. Essentially, what I suggest is that neoliberalism is more than one movement among the others in conservative modernization; it is, in large part, *the* movement, in its authoritarianism, from which the others take their cue.

Neoliberalism

Concentration of wealth tends to be a result of the supply-side economics inherent in neoliberalism relying on massive tax cuts for the wealthy such that, as the theory goes, capital will "trickle down." Even more specific to my purposes, and a point to which I return, is that it involves private takeover of once public goods, including education. Here I must emphasize that such "takeover" occurs not only through the overt privatization of heretofore public institutions but also through ideological hegemony and the covert takeover of public institutions in terms of the ways that they function and the policies and practices to which teachers and students are subjected. Schools are effectively victims of both kinds of takeover: the former through the increase in the number of for-profit, "public" schools, for example, and the latter through the standards and accountability movement.[1]

As Steger and Roy (2010) put it, "Neoliberalism functions as an ideology, a mode of governance, and a policy package emphasizing the pivotal role of free markets and private enterprise" (p. 136). In this way, neoliberalism includes more than a general sense of hyper-capitalism that often accompanies such discussions. Its functioning as an ideology is consistent with the work of Olssen and Peters (2005) for whom neoliberalism acts as a political rationality that offers a "worked out discourse containing theories and ideas that emerge in response to concrete problems within a determined historical period" (p. 315). These "concrete problems" are attended to by a series of sociopolitical solutions driven by four key values: hyper-individualism, hyper-surveillance, economic determinants of productivity, and competitive entrepreneurialism (Kuntz, 2015).

Neoliberalism is new because it is a dramatic change from the Keynesian economics that dominated the post-depression era. As George (1999) argues, "In 1945 or 1950, if you had seriously proposed any of the ideas and policies in today's standard neoliberal toolkit, you would have been laughed off the stage or sent off to the insane asylum" (para 2). However, when stagflation set in the 1970s (and earlier), exacerbated by the oil crises of the same period, the stage was set for the new ideology to take hold. Building on the idea of the materially self-interested, consumptive, competitive, and profiteering *homo economicus*, "neoliberals call for the employment of governmental technologies that are taken from the world of business and commerce" "rather than operating along more traditional lines of pursuing the public good (rather than profits) by enhancing civil society and social justice" (Steger & Roy, 2010, p. 12).

The authoritarianism of neoliberalism, noted previously, derives, as David Harvey (2005) points out, from the paradox of the necessity of state intervention necessary to impose neoliberal reforms. Neoliberal authoritarianism functions through state apparati that emphasize austerity and privatization. Starving public agencies not only creates the conditions for their ultimate failure but also legitimizes private takeover, a process that Harvey, updating Marx's notion of primitive accumulation, terms "accumulation by dispossession." Similar to the closing of feudal commons, profits accrue to the capitalist through the privatization of public resources through coercion. Financial coercion through austerity represents such violence that neoliberalism can no longer be seen as just ideological, it is a material arm of government that manufactures social crisis requiring yet more austerity, control, laws, and policies to maintain the order.[2] Here, then, we see all three notions of fixity coming together: Neoliberal policies pretend to address a social crisis (repair) while reinscribing neoliberalism (stasis) which becomes a common sense fix through ideology (manipulation, as in "the fix is in").

(Neo)Conservatism and Authoritarian Populists

Historically, conservativism, deriving from classical Liberalism, followed a certain amount of libertarianism in terms of social and cultural issues and a commitment to laissez faire capitalism in terms of economic policy. Certainly modern conservatives have been more willing than modern liberals to restrict individual rights while promoting economic rights. However, in the United States, conservativism took a sharper right turn upon the election of Ronald Reagan and there was a similar turn in the UK with the ascension of Margaret Thatcher to the prime ministership. This right turn ushered in a new brand of conservative, the neoconservative. As their conservative peers, neoconservatives retain the commitment to laissez faire capitalism, free trade, corporate power and big business, and the economic freedom to sell one's labor power as one sees fit. However, the libertarian impulse inherent in (paleo)conservativism on social issues and individual freedom, that is, civil rights, was lost. Neoconservatives are content for government to play a much more intrusive role not only in solidarity with neoliberals to maintain economic policy but also in the life of individuals. This is typically justified in the name of public security, patriotism, and "traditional" values. This emphasis on law and moral order takes on a collectivist positioning, antithetical to the classical Liberalism from which contemporary conservativism derived. As Kuntz et al. write, neoconservatives situate government as a protector of what is "sacred about the state—the shared values that hold it together" (p. 490).

In many ways, neoconservativism in the United States took its lead from whom Apple (2006) calls authoritarian populists, members of the Christian right. As he explains it, "authoritarian populists ground their positions on education and social policy in general in particular visions of biblical authority" (p. 44). Apropos to this, influential Baptist Minister Jerry Falwell noted, "We're fighting a holy war… What's happened to America is that the wicked are bearing rule." Thus, Falwell believed it is his duty "to apply the truths of Scripture to every act of government" (cited in Banwart, 2013). With the concurrence of fellow "Christian" leader, Pat Robertson, Falwell, in response to the 9/11 terrorist attacks, grotesquely opined, "The pagans and the abortionists and the feminists and the gays and the lesbians who are actively trying to make that an alternative lifestyle, the ACLU, People for the American Way—all of them who have tried to secularize America, I point the finger in their face and say 'you helped this happen'" (Goodstein, 2001). More currently, as he rejects equal pay for women and supports conversion therapy for LGBT people, the Falwellian anti-feminist and anti-gay views of Vice President Mike Pence are well known.

Given such viewpoints, it should come as no surprise that what might count as legitimate knowledge (e.g., evolution) and democratic values (e.g., questioning) in schools might come under attack. Here conservatives and neoconservatives alike frequently join the authoritarian populist clamor for scripture and a "return" to traditional morality while adding demands that "traditional" knowledge and unquestionable "truths" drive school curricula (despite their more recent reliance on "alternative facts").[3] They cast such things as peace studies, gender studies, and multiculturalism as superficial distractions from "real" knowledge while maligning their defenders as "cultural relativists," "ideologues," "ignorant activists," "antipatriotic," and "threats to liberty" (Kornfeld, 2005). Importantly, however, the very religious values that remain foundational to authoritarian populism remain tied to an economic rationale of development: "A meaningful and productive life is one that is economical viable …. thus the values-driven logic of authoritarian populism finds traction in the economic sphere" (Kuntz et al., p. 490).

Nevertheless, curricular reform does not stop at the double-teaming provided by the neoconservative/authoritarian populist agenda. Neoliberal educational reform, while focusing at the policy level writ large in terms of implementing corporate-competitive models of school improvement in the form of charter schools and vouchers, also directs curricular reform. Neoliberal curricular reform is focused on the student (read: client) as human capital. In Sweden, for example, a national initiative began in 2009 to permeate curricular reform with the idea of entrepreneurship (Nordin & Sundberg, 2014). As "entrepreneurship" is interpreted and implemented differently at the school level (van Dijk & Mensch, 2015), such neoliberal initiatives may not "permeate" school curricula in the same way. However, they do provide an overriding ethos that reinscribes the dominant neoliberal order while, therefore, also dictating what curricular content makes sense.

Illustrative here are recent discussions in Texas about curricular standards which stress the importance of capitalism. As Petrovic and Kuntz (2014) explain, in Texas,

> not only are non-capitalistic economic models absent in the K–8 standards, but also the ability to critique, an important intellectual capacity in a democracy supposedly based on rational deliberation among competing ideals, is missing. For example,

students are expected to "explain how government regulations and taxes impact consumer costs," but not how the profit motive does. Students are to "identify historical figures, such as individuals, past and present, including Henry Ford, and other entrepreneurs in the community such as Mary Kay Ash, and Wallace Amos, Milton Hershey, and Sam Walton, and ordinary people in the community who have started new businesses." At the high school level, "The student understands the historical origins of contemporary economic systems and the benefits of free enterprise in world history." (p. xii)

It seems uncontroversial to observe from this that "schools remain largely places of highly regulated transmission" (Boxley, p. 110). In this vein, in both of these reforms from Sweden and the United States, I see the overlap between conservatives, neoconservatives, and neoliberals to the extent that traditional, accepted "knowledge" assumes that capitalism is not only the only objectively correct economic system ("There is no alternative," as Margaret Thatcher famously put it) but also the ideal that must be sold as truth—objective, common sense content—in schools and exported as such around the world. Indeed, in foreign policy—especially as I see it in US foreign policy as carried out by US puppet organizations such as the IMF and the World Bank—the exportation of free market, neoliberal ideals becomes a patriotic duty, more than an economic theory but a value system of economic freedom that undergirds interpretations of democracy. Thus, as suggested previously, neoliberalism is more than a movement in conservative modernization; it is the driving force.

Mapping Fixity

In the previous section, I sought to define the different forces of conservative modernization, offering some examples as to how they manifest. Here, I want to get back to an explanation of the processes of fixity which, in the neoliberal order, always manifest simultaneously as repair, stasis, and manipulation. Indeed, in this order, repair is the rhetorical device that manipulates into action the fix that is stasis, that is, a protection of the status quo or movement to nowhere. It might be argued that these forces are not static, as they do move us to embrace even more radical neoliberal reforms. But, this, it seems to me, is what I have defined as fixity—when the so-called movement simply strengthens those forces that called for the particular movement in the first place.

In the neoliberal order, solutions to perceived social problems/concerns are approached through the logic of the market. As such, social institutions, including schools, are framed as businesses. A plaintive example was provided by the Ontario Minister of Education in 1995 who argued that "In primary and secondary education, the client is the student and the customer is the taxpayer and the parent.... I believe [in] (*sic*) a Ministry of Education that is clear about the *business* it is in" (cited in Pinto, 2012, p. 56, emphasis added). Moreover, as we saw in the examples from Sweden and Texas above, the neoliberal project is not only to treat and run schools as businesses but also to educate students for business. From this perspective, the ideals of "public" education and a liberal arts education that do not seek to fit children into the economic machinery become problems to be fixed. Laura Pinto (2012) notes that "at the heart of framing Ontario's [neoliberal] school reform during the 1990s were struggles over what, if any, education problems needed to be 'fixed'" (p. 53), and neoliberalism provides a large toolkit of fixes to repair schools. These include—according to mandatory development of strategic plans and risk management—the creation of surpluses, cost–benefit analysis and other efficiency calculations, the shrinking of political governance, the setting of quantitative targets, the close monitoring of outcomes, the creation of highly individualized performance-based work plans, and the introduction of rational choice models that internalize and thus normalize market-oriented behavior (Steger & Roy, 2010).

Such fixes begin to name the four elements mentioned previously, especially economic productivity and competitive entrepreneurialism. Again, with such governing tactics, the notion of fix as repair collapses into fix as stasis. First, normalizing market behavior creates market subjects, holding in place an unquestioned neoliberal order which occludes and, in fact, disallows other subjectivities. Market subjects, as commodities, must have their value measured.

Measurability manifests as hyper-surveillance which requires student-subjects to make themselves visible through quantifiable determinations of value; the subject always already recognizable through a series of linked points of data. This, of course, is accountability to measure the achievement of standards so overtly missing for the neoconservative. But, furthermore, for the neoliberal, these intersecting data-points (the subject) are granted value through their potential to predict *economic productivity*, a key value that marks subjects as useful citizens. Lastly, *competitive entrepreneurialism* extends values of individual advancement in social standing over alterations at the level of the group (or class). In this sense, "progress" is an individual endeavor, not a collective goal.

Adding to and connecting Steger and Roy's examples directly to the construction of students, these four neoliberal elements drive policies that, for example, value standardized tests for their ability to do all of the following: define students absent social context (of poverty, for example, or historical disenfranchisement); make individual students visible via a conglomerate of intersecting data-points (such as SAT/ACT scores, GPA, etc.); predict student achievement in relation to economic output (the ability to take on school loans, for example, or gain a degree that is recognizable in the job market); and mark select students for advancement over their peers (consider in this case "Honors" or "Advanced" curricular tracks in schools). Such fixes not only drive but also reproduce the neoliberal order through and by a neoliberal model of schooling.

The values and assumptions in this order are simultaneously normalized and normalizing, constructing educational institutions as havens for bureaucracy. They are attended to by bureaucrats (those who are "concerned with the order of society, the well-being of the population and the training of citizens") and producing a bureaucratic citizenry ("someone who detaches him/herself from ethical and political…commitments in order to be able to be involved in the administration of the population") (Simons, Masschelein, & Quaghebeur, 2005, p. 821). Schooling becomes an extended bureaucratic process with devastating effects on any possibility for education to fulfill an activating function for a more democratic future. Such bureaucrats exemplify what Apple (2006) refers to as the managerial middle class. The growth of managerialism owes much to increasing privatization whether of traditionally public services such as school transportation or remedial services or of increased infiltration of private companies into school-profiteering as in the testing industry (test development, test preparation services, test analyses, etc.) (Burch, 2009).

The massive growth of what can only be called the testing-industrial-complex is simultaneously an outgrowth of and reproductive of neoliberalism. As Foucault (2003) has noted, contemporary manifestations of neoliberalism require a comparative capacity that links individuals to larger formations of population, resulting in the ability to govern through statistical relations that situate singular data-points against larger conglomerates of data-groups. Through this relation, assertions of normalcy and deviancy (or, in discussion of identity, pathology) take on material dimensions, resulting in a host of daily practices designed to replicate the status quo against alternative possibilities of being otherwise. Of course, the system succeeds in replicating its own logic through determining which practices or processes are worthy of notation (as data) and which are not identifiable and therefore outside any relational capacity. The end result is a self-reinforcing process of governmentality that has led Ben Baez (2014) to deem ours a *society of the statistic.*

Such technologies of stasis necessarily impact curricula not only as a neoliberal project but now also as a (neo)conservative one. Now curriculum must not only align to that which is measurable, but also the measurable is squared against traditional "knowledge" in the neoconservative order. Thus, these components of conservative modernization work to maintain the social status quo by measuring a sentimental relation to the past—a type of imperialist nostalgia first articulated by Rosaldo (1993). As a consequence, educational systems take on the necrophilic characteristics noted by Fromm (1973): "the past is experienced as quite real, not the present or the future. What has been, i.e. what is dead, rules…the past is sacred…drastic change is a crime against the natural order" (p. 339). What has been remains the focal point for the necrophilic institution as any allusion to a future possibility calls forth an ambiguity that is simply not tolerated by the normative logic that dominates our contemporary moment.

This necrophilic tendency manifests in the curriculum wars. As Apple (2006) describes them, neoconservatives are guided by "a romantic appraisal of the past…a 'return' to higher standards, a revivification of the 'Western tradition,' patriotism, and conservative variants of character education" (p. 39). A stark example of this is captured in the documentary *Precious Knowledge.* The video documents the fate of the Mexican American Studies program in Tucson, AZ, schools. Deemed to be illegal via a law written specifically to make it so, the program was shut down even as an independent evaluation not only contradicted the "legal" conclusion but also found the program to be highly effective academically. In the video, then State Superintendent of Public Instruction, John Huppenthal, condemns the program for "trashing the founding fathers," since during a classroom visit by Huppenthal someone had commented that Benjamin Franklin had been a racist. Historical accuracy was less important than ideological commitment for Huppenthal and other "leaders" in Arizona. Similarly, recall the curricular changes in Texas that exemplify the overlap between the neoconservative and the neoliberal. The curricular standards there emphasize capitalism in a way that can only rightly be called indoctrination (Petrovic & Kuntz, 2014). In such examples, we see the sacredness of the past and an absoluteness of truth, an absoluteness within which ambiguity and the critical thinking it might generate are simply intolerable.

Thus, we see interconnectedness of the fixity inherent to conservative modernization. Neoliberalism requires accountability and measurability and measurability requires truth or, at least, the illusion of objectivity. In turn, the objective truths are magically found in a sacred past. This sacred past is now said to include the neoliberal order. The fix is in.

Finding the Liberal in the Neoliberal

Given this status quo, the question that necessarily arises is "what is the end we seek in *un*fixing schools?" This speaks to the age-old question of the purpose of schools. While any number of broad purposes might be listed—economic, social, intellectual, political, personal—we come back to some of the fundamental ideals of the Liberal democratic state. Principal among these ideals are freedom, autonomy, and the ability to lead a flourishing life. These ideals cannot be served in any robust sense by the kind of fixity that manifests in conservative modernization.

These, of course, are ideals core to what is typically referred to as classical Liberalism and are ideals that (neo)liberals, (neo)conservatives, and even authoritarian populists all generally claim to hold dear—even as contradictions abound. Arguably, a keystone of such contradictions is set by another fundamental notion of classical Liberalism: economic freedom in the sense of being able to sell one's labor power as he or she sees fit. This is especially true of neoliberalism which has upped the ante in free market discourse. The underlying assumption here is that people are best motivated by financial incentive which then justifies the laissez faire, free market system in which the "invisible hand" will ensure economic justice. The role of government, a minimalist government, in this conceptualization is to ensure citizens' negative freedoms. Of course, neoliberals rhetorically claim but practically reject a minimalist government since neoliberalism requires quite deliberate state intervention to sell itself.

More contemporarily, the principle of laissez faire came under greater scrutiny as Liberal political philosophers and economists sought to tackle the unjust excesses of capitalism. John Maynard Keynes (1936), for example, saw no reason that the government should not intervene in the economy in the form of spending on public works in order to employ the unemployed. He also believed that wages should remain stable, against the dominant idea that wages might be cut to benefit output. Subsequently, John Rawls (1971) reinvigorated the debate in his *Theory of Justice* in which he defends a form of liberal egalitarianism. As Keynes, Rawls seeks to address the excesses of capitalism, in his case through what he called the "difference principle." By this principle, any social and economic inequalities are justified only if they are to the advantage of the least well off. Rawls' theory of justice was a response to utilitarians and, of course, generated responses of its own, most famously from Robert Nozick (1974) (from a right-libertarian position) and also from more thorough-going (radical) egalitarians such as Kai Nielsen (1985) who argued that Rawls' theory of justice simply collapsed into utilitarianism.

A full review of these works is not necessary to the point here, which is that, while still debatable perhaps, what these debates establish is that economic freedom as argued in radical-right approaches (by the likes of, for example, Friedrich Hayek, Robert Nozick, Milton Friedman, Ayn Rand, etc.) is not the end all and be all of Liberalism. Rawls' more egalitarian approach, for example, while not making an argument against capitalism, highlights the necessity of egalitarianism to ensure the social cooperation necessary for all people to lead a good life, especially given the arbitrariness of one's social position. Thus, I focus on the Liberal principles listed above as guiding in Liberal political theory while eschewing the historic focus on economic freedom as such, which, I insist, does not make the approach illiberal. I should also note that while Liberalism is by no means the only way or the best way to inform work toward a just society and more democratic educational policies and practices, it does provide a common language in Western-style democracies to gain purchase for reform. In short, just as Freire (1985) argued that we cannot be afraid to use the word democracy, I am suggesting that critical pedagogues must claim Liberalism in a way that serves democracy.

Freedom

In Liberal political theory, the ideal of freedom derived directly from a view of human nature wherein people are born in a state of perfect freedom. Thus Liberalism turns on the notion that societal institutions should serve the end of the freedom of individuals, individuals being the basis of society. Should restrictions against individual freedoms be deemed necessary, this necessity must be proven by those who seek to limit those freedoms and that such limits must be "only for the public good" (Locke, 1823, p. 195). Thus, freedom is the non-restriction of options to the extent that the option one might choose does not interfere with the freedom of others to pursue their options. This is principally a notion of negative freedom.

We see the defense of negative freedom, and negative freedom only, in libertarian positions such as that of Nozick (1974). Here the role of the state should be minimal: "the night-watchman state of classical Liberal theory" which is "limited to the functions of protecting all its citizens against violence, theft, and fraud, and to the enforcement of contracts, and so on …" (Nozick, p. 26). This notion has a long history famously invoked in John Stuart Mill's (1871/2002) harm principle: "That the only purpose for which power can be rightfully exercised over any member of a civilised community, against his will, is to prevent harm to others" (p. 8). In short, negative freedom refers to a simple absence of interference and freedom from coercion. Isaiah Berlin (1969) is worth citing at some length here; he writes,

> I am normally said to be free to the degree to which no man or body of men interferes with my activity. Political liberty in this sense is simply the area within which a man can act unobstructed by others. If I am prevented by others from doing what I could otherwise do, I am to that degree unfree; and if this area is contracted by other men beyond a certain minimum, I can be described as being coerced, or, it may be, enslaved. Coercion is not, however, a term that covers every form of inability. If I say that I am unable to jump more than ten feet in the air, or cannot read because I am blind…it would be eccentric to say that I am to that degree enslaved or coerced. Coercion implies the deliberate interference of other human beings within the area in which I could otherwise act. You lack political liberty or freedom only if you are prevented from attaining a goal by other human beings. (p. 122)

As I will elaborate in Chapter 3, it is the case that in schools children lack even this most basic notion of freedom. There is the frequent prohibition or restriction of movement, the prohibition or restriction of communication, the prohibition or restriction of choice, etc. The coveted hall pass acts as a restriction even of basic bodily function. Increasingly, of course, even the so-called free time of such things as recess are being reduced. Kids cannot learn to be free when unfree for most of their time.

This idea of negative freedom has, of course, its inverse: positive freedom.

Positive Freedom or Autonomy

The freedom to pursue one's activities requires, of course, the rational capacity to determine what those activities should be and what version of the good life one should pursue. In other words, it requires autonomy wherein to regard oneself as autonomous "a person must see himself as sovereign in deciding what to believe and in weighing competing reasons for action" (Scanlon, 1972, pp. 215–216). Scanlon goes on to argue that the autonomous person, while she might consider the judgments of others, must, in the end, demonstrate independence of reason in terms of deciding which judgments and subsequent actions might be correct and why. Appositively, this requires "the capacity for critical self-reflection in the development of value systems and plans of action" (Christman, 2005, p. 87). Such conceptualizations of autonomy are what Berlin (1969) refers to as positive freedom.

Positive freedom is presented as the *freedom to* conceive of, develop, and pursue one's goals. It is the sense of being one's own master, "to be moved by reasons, by conscious purposes which are my own, not by causes which affect me, as it were, from outside" (Berlin, 1969, p. 161). Note that the notion of *freedom to* might be confusing to the extent that it can be interpreted as addressing the question of whether or not I can act on the choices I make, whether or not the conditions exist such that I may do so. For now it should be made clear that the notion of positive freedom posited by Berlin might be more accurately termed autonomy as defined previously. Compare, for example, Christman's definition of autonomy above with Berlin's further description of positive freedom as being "conscious of myself as a thinking, willing, active being, bearing responsibility for his choices and able to explain them by reference to his own ideas and purposes" (Berlin, 1969, p. 161).

Connecting the ideal of autonomy or positive freedom with the determination of what is correct, Rawls argues,

> It is in their public recognition and informed application of the principles of justice in their political life, and as their effective sense of justice directs, that citizens achieve full autonomy. Thus, full autonomy is realized by citizens when they act from principles of justice that specify the fair terms of cooperation they would give to themselves when fairly represented as free and equal persons. (p. 77)

Rawls' notion of "full autonomy" seems to capture and rely on both negative and positive freedom.

Winch (2006) suggests that "a society's education system is one of the key means through which individuals become autonomous" (p. 1). Certainly, this *should* be the case. But the suggestion that it *is* the case must be challenged. Again, fixed schools, just as they function against the understanding and experience of negative freedom, are problematic to the development of positive freedom. Springer, Lopes de Souza, and White (2016) bring together my concerns regarding both negative and positive freedom in schools:

> Schooling perpetuates the myth of freedom by attempting to convince us that we are on an emancipatory path, that we are transforming our lives by learning. Unfortunately, the fix is in. How are we free when there is no improvisation and the script has been written for us? What do we actually learn when we are temporally regulated and spatially confined? How much autonomy do we have when someone decides for us what is important, legitimate, useful, and accepted knowledge? (p. 9)

So here we must consider, somewhat paradoxically, the development of autonomy within the material conditions of school that undermine autonomy. If autonomy must, negatively, preclude manipulation or, positively, require sovereignty, then, schools as they currently exist, do not provide the space for its development. But there remains some notion of autonomy as described above that education must pursue.

Flourishing and Effective Autonomy

Both freedom and autonomy are required for citizens to lead a flourishing life. The question of what constitutes "a flourishing life" is a perennial one, tracing back, at least, to the idea of the examined life of Socrates. The examined life and its connection to flourishing are made explicitly in Aristotle's *Nicomachean Ethics*. To live as *eudaimon* (a flourishing person) or achieve the objective state (for Aristotle) of *eudaimonism* is to function within the rational part of the soul. As Kraut (2018) summarizes Aristotle, "The good of a human being must have something to do with being human; and what sets humanity off from other species, giving us the potential to live a better life, is our capacity to guide ourselves by using reason. If we use reason well, we live well as human beings; or, to be more precise, using reason well over the course of a full life is what happiness consists in" (para. 7).

As can be seen, reason and, hence, autonomy are inherent, certainly, to the life worth living. But, the idea of flourishing strikes as an even more robust position. Contemporarily, Harry Brighouse (2000, especially chapter 4; 2006) takes up this line of thinking. While autonomy plays an inherently important role in enabling people to lead flourishing lives, in order for a life to be flourishing it must, first, contain objectively valuable goods and must be lived from the inside. Of course, as Brighouse acknowledges, identifying which goods may or may not be "objectively valuable" is controversial. But certainly it eliminates some objectively unworthwhile or outright bad things such as a life devoted to hoarding money (Brighouse's example, 2006) or finding happiness in harming others. Second, a flourishing life must be lived from the inside. In other words, a person's conception of the good for herself, her reasons for and plans of action, must be based on her examined interests, desires, hopes, and fears. But it is important to point out also that flourishing is not just about the good for oneself but also for others because each of our "interests are bound up with those of other people" (Brighouse, 2006, p. 20).

In a basic way, Brighouse's notion of flourishing is a slightly expanded notion of autonomy. However, the commitment here to understanding how one's interests are bound with those of other people is an important step away from the hyper-individualism that has become a hallmark of contemporary Liberalism, exacerbated by the construction of *homo economicus*. Relatedly, Hewitt (2005) points out that there is no such thing as freedom in general. First, of course, we are always limited by the sociopolitical context, rules, regulations, laws, the gaze, etc. But, I think more importantly to my purposes here, freedom is relational. In terms of autonomy, we become who we are and understand our choices by understanding the choices of others. We cannot, therefore, reach the transcendental freedom of Kant, for example; we are not autonomous choosers. We do not simply choose to be; we become. This said, within this becoming, we must certainly behave as if something like autonomous choice or free will exists. The point of education then, as White (2002) puts it, is to provide students "with whatever acquaintance is necessary with a wide range of possible intrinsic goods from which to make informed choices" (p. 445). But this must still be taken relationally and within the material contexts, which students must also come to understand. Thus, making such choices is still about becoming within such relations. And, it is the being in relation to others that capitalist social relations pervert through the material conditions it creates.

Here Brighouse spends important, but too little, time on commercialism and financial concerns, given the contemporary neoliberal order. He importantly notes that, "The striking feature of commercialism in culture is that not only are the values that commercial interests promote not good values, but also the people promoting them do not believe them to be good" (p. 49). The juxtaposition of the values of commercialism and the values of flourishing was brought into startling relief on February 4, 2018 during the Super Bowl game. The date is significant as the commercial begins with words on the screen:

Dr. Martin Luther King, Jr.
February 4, 1968
Spoken 50 years ago
Today

The commercial then proceeds with an actual recording of one of Martin Luther King, Jr.'s speeches. It seems, unsurprisingly, to speak directly to the concept of flourishing: "He who is greatest among you, shall be your servant." The greatest servant in this particular commercial, it turns out, is a Ram truck, brought to you by Chrysler. Presumably, the greatest way to serve is to purchase one.

The problem of commercialism is a growing concern in cash-strapped schools forced to accept or even seek out corporate support. An example is provided from Pittsburgh in the documentary *Captive Audience* (Jhally, 2003). In Pittsburgh, the school district considered entering an exclusive soda contract with PepsiCo. The district backed out of the plan when it was revealed that the school would have to *double* student consumption of Pepsi products during the school day. The district would end up owing the difference to PepsiCo if not. Here commercialism is not merely a bad value, but, as noted by Alex Molnar in the video, it is linked to dangerous behavior as increasing numbers of young people face the onset of serious type II diabetes. In these types of neoliberal manipulations, shopping is sold directly as freedom. And, if you aren't convinced, you can get a "Freedom" Visa from Chase (0% Introductory APR).

Obviously, commercialism—i.e., selling shopping—is directly related to the financial complexities of modern society. Indebtedness is encouraged even as most people lead increasingly precarious economic lives. Indeed, the new term "precariat" captures the precariousness of the economic lives of the proletariat (Chomsky, 2016). Thus, the real problem here is the lack of a reasonable equality of condition. I will leave for another time the consideration of what is "reasonable" here. However, a certain level of equality of condition is required for *effective freedom*. Much like positive freedom earlier, effective freedom is a form of "freedom to." Effective freedom refers to freedoms, opportunities, and/or "rights" that are not just formally available but actually and meaningfully actionable. Certainly, the pursuit, as some would have it, of negative freedom alone results in grossly disparate life chances and a certain level of equality of condition is necessary for equality (cf. Nielsen, 1985; Rawls, 1971). For Nielsen "substantive legal and political equality [are] in reality importantly dependent on economic factors" and, therefore, formal legal and political equality "are not nearly sufficient conditions for equality" (p. 6). Nielsen's point is to provide a certain level of equality of condition in order to lessen the huge differences in life prospects—because of power, authority, or privilege over others—that we currently see. The promotion of the moral power to determine one's vision of the good life—autonomy—is meaningless if that vision is not pursuable.

Where the bottom 20% of earners spend nearly two-thirds (63.7%) of their income meeting basic needs (housing, food, healthcare), the top 20% of earners is able to spend five times more (as percentage of income) on personal insurance and pensions. The top 20% also spends five and a half times more on education in real dollars, even as the bottom spends close to the same amount as a percentage of their income (Morrell & Kiersz, 2017). Without some kind of support, the hours it takes the poor and working class merely to survive cannot equate to effective opportunity, not to mention the leisure that Brighouse also suggests is necessary to flourishing.

Even as a notion of effective freedom is not a value in classical Liberal political theory, it seems to me that such a notion is required to render freedom and autonomy valuable. To demonstrate how income level creates "bottlenecks" in opportunity, Fishkin (2014) addresses a "hypothetical" "America." In this America, "money buys too much of what matters. Money is needed to buy too much that cuts too close to the core of what any person with a plausible conception of the good life would value" (p. 201). It seems clear to me that Fishkin uses "hypothetical" figuratively, as he describes the current state of affairs quite accurately: where basic healthcare costs money, where one needs to live in a middle-class or wealthier neighborhood to have reasonably good schools, where preschool and daycare and college all cost a lot, and where layoff, pay cuts, and benefits can be easily cut toward the maintenance of the precariat. It is notable that Fishkin's "hypothetical" counterexample in this section is "Denmark."

Of course, neoliberals, like classical liberals, would balk at the state interference required to create the conditions necessary for effective freedom to obtain. But notice that state interference does not seem to be the real concern here. The real concern is the ideological shifts: from greed to sharing or from competitiveness to cooperation. After all, markets must be marketed. As I noted above, commercialism is about selling shopping as freedom. Creating the conditions for such values to thrive requires a large, powerful state to keep democracy and the people at bay such that corporations might prosper.

Thus, neoliberalism moves away from the negative ideal of freedom in classical Liberalism to its own brand of effective freedom, that is, the creation of the conditions necessary to inculcate the ideological, cultural, and spiritual domination of the market and the concomitant profiteering and creation of the precariat.

Moving Away from the Illiberal Limits of Conservative Modernization

In short, the basic Liberal ideals discussed above—freedom, autonomy, and flourishing—cannot be served in any robust sense by the kind of fixity that manifests in conservative modernization. This is especially true as the neoliberal driver of conservative modernization precipitates gross inequality, undermining the effective freedom necessary to flourishing. Conservative modernization involves a number of commitments—axiological (e.g., authoritarian populist totalizing views of the good life), epistemological (e.g., neoconservative renderings of truth), and ideological (e.g., neoliberal commitment to capitalism). Each of these involves a political battle of one kind or another in shaping policy and a vision for society. Schooling takes shape accordingly.

Given this, it is imperative to understand, especially vis-à-vis neoliberalism, that bourgeois education is education in class and that the project is, therefore, always already political. Schools, as I will discuss in greater detail in Chapter 3, are ideological state apparatuses. Thus, the left cannot call out the right as being political and propose some sort of depoliticization of schools. Given the dominant ideology driven by conservative modernization, this has always been a much more effective tactic for conservatives, who can dismiss the left as socialist ideologues. The point here is not to make education any more or less political but to rescue it from the politics of neoliberal hegemony, turning it toward transformative ends. This we cannot do, as Lenin pointed out, by "conduct[ing] educational work in isolation from politics" (cited in Boxley, 2017, p. 113).

Despite this rather bleak discussion, I, as other resistance theorists before me, see in the materiality of schooling space where productive change might occur—instances where one might provocatively *unfix* schooling, thereby disrupting its fixity and necrophilic tendencies. This requires a politics of resistance, not isolation from politics. Given this, it is important to note how critical scholars in the past have sought to address educational possibility amidst our increasingly neoliberal times. Therefore, in the chapters to follow I discuss two such attempts to "unfix" schooling: critical pedagogy and unschooling. Though both examples extend from similar critiques of education as colluding with normative values and practices toward violently conservative ends, I will conclude that they also misread the material contexts in which schooling is enacted, unnecessarily shortchanging the disruptive power of their critique.

Notes

1. In Chapter 3, I discuss the process of the takeover of public institutions and the increase in Educational Management Organizations. In Chapter 4, I present a specific example of how neoliberal logic affects teaching practices, ultimately "educating" students to the neoliberal order.
2. It is, for example, no accident that prison expansion correlates with austerity measures such as welfare reform (Wacquant, 2009, cited in Azar).
3. In a television interview on the US show "Meet the Press," January 22, 2017, Kellyanne Conway, conservative spokesperson and advisor to President Trump, used the expression "alternative facts" to defend a demonstrable falsehood stated by then White House Press Secretary, Sean Spicer. In this vein, there was an interesting discursive shift in the campaigns of Democrats and Republicans in the US Presidential election in 2016. Where the left has typically been about seeing other perspectives (a la critical pedagogy and questioning), the right has been about Truth. In 2016, the left was left asking, "What happened to truth?"

· 2 ·

UNFIXING EDUCATION WITH CRITICAL PEDAGOGY

This chapter provides a discussion of the roots of critical pedagogy and general role of schools from a Marxian perspective. Here I note why critical pedagogy must embrace Marxism as a means to promote social justice and flourishing against the reproductive role of schools and conservative forces. This necessarily includes reinvigorating the development of autonomy in students and the capacity to lead flourishing lives. Within this general review of the Marxist foundation, history, approach, and hope of critical pedagogy, I begin this chapter with a discussion of Marx's materialist conception of history. While they were not orthodox Marxists, Marx did, of course, inspire the critical theory pursued by members of the Frankfurt School—led by Max Horkheimer.[1] Critical theory, in turn, provides the foundation for critical pedagogy. Thus, I review each of these subsequent to the review of Marxism.

Each of these reviews points back to the previous discussion of how neoliberalism fixes education, now, from a Marxian perspective, toward the end of reinscribing extant social relations of production. Foreshadowing a deeper analysis in Chapter 3, I conclude in this chapter that critical pedagogy, even as a particular outgrowth of Marxism, fails to take on the materialist challenge to institutions. Even so, I agree that "Class is the salient form of structural oppression within capitalist society, it is the inevitable and defining feature of capitalist exploitation, whereas the various other forms of oppression are not essential to its nature and continuation, however much they are commonly functional to this" (Boxley, p. 64). Thus, it remains crucial to any reconsideration of critical pedagogy to begin with orthodox Marxism, understanding that "a critical reflexive Marxist theory...can prove foundational in the development of...pedagogies of liberation" (McLaren & Farahmnadpur, 2000, p. 28). In other words, undermining this most salient form of inequality—class—carries with it an ethos of egalitarian politics more generally.

Orthodox Marxism

It is commonly understood that critical pedagogy is an outgrowth of critical theory. Critical theory, in turn, traces back to orthodox Marxism even as proponents of the former reinterpret some central notions of the latter. Given the previously stated conclusion, it is incumbent upon me to provide an understanding of orthodox Marxism. Crucial here is the important influence of Hegel on Marx, especially concerning several key concepts, including the dialectic, materialism, and alienation.[2]

In perhaps his most important contribution to critical theory, Hegel develops his notion of the dialectic that forms self-consciousness, of being for oneself, through and with the other. As Hegel writes,

> Thus the relation of the two self-conscious individuals is such that they prove themselves and each other through a life-and-death struggle. They must engage in this struggle, for they must raise their certainty of being *for themselves* to truth, both in the case of the other and in their own case. (p. 114, emphasis in original)

Famously, Hegel casts this struggle as between lord and bondsman. This has commonly been referred to as the master/slave dialectic. Nevertheless, it is important to understand the relationship in Hegel's terms given his focus on German feudalism (Cole, 2005; Duquette, 2002). The relationship of lord to bondsman illustrates the dialectic as a process of becoming through the contradictions of the relationship. Foremost among these contradictions is the resultant dependence of lord upon the bondsman. Of course, the outcome of this contradiction is not the reversal of roles, but freeing the bondsman from his servitude.

Again, the context of German feudalism, the primary structures of which were still in place in Hegel's time, is key to understanding Hegel's dialectic. This is because, as Cole (2005) argues, the relationship between lord and bondsman derives from a "dialectic of possession." The ambiguity of "ownership" in feudal conditions created competing claims by the serf whose claim rested on his working the land, the lord whose claim rested on managing the land, the monarch who granted the lands, etc. It is the struggle for possession and the contradictions between different kinds of possessing (e.g., vs. owning) that drives the lord/bondsman dialectic. The desire to possess, in this case to possess the land, leads to the desire to possess one's self. And, as indicated in the previous quote from Hegel, the self is found not only in the one but also in the other.

On the one hand, there is no denying Hegel's idealism: Human history is the development of consciousness and it is reason that advances freedom. On the other hand, Hegel's care toward contextualization makes him "more presciently Marxist than what his critics have allowed" (Cole, 2005, p. 584; see Gibson's (2006) discussion of Hegel as an example). This debate, in its particularities, is somewhat of a sidebar and my point is not to enter it per se but to observe the strong influence of Hegel on Marx and, therefore, the importance of Hegel in reviving critical pedagogy, both for his positive and negative influences. Clearly, Hegel sets a foundation for Marx's materialism which arguably derives neatly from Hegel's idealism or, at least, from the way that Hegel argues his idealism by drawing on German feudalism.

Furthermore, it is German feudalism that provides Hegel his entrée into the discussion of alienation, another important concept upon which Marx builds. While alienation may seem a negative process, it is key to the phenomenological development of consciousness and, therefore, a necessary if not positive aspect. For it is the very experience of alienation that allows consciousness to overcome alienation (Rae, 2012). A primary form of experience for Hegel was work. Work is an invaluable function of that which makes us human and, therefore, is liberating. This was what Hegel referred to as "natural labor" (cf. Cole, 2005). This was "the labour of the individual for his own needs" (Hegel, 1977, p. 213). Hegel also saw that work as largely creative of an externalized world for the worker, which was inherent and inescapable. This was because

> The labour of the individual for his own needs is just as much a satisfaction of the needs of others as of his own, and the satisfaction of his own needs he only obtains through the labour of others. As the individual in his individual work already unconsciously performs a universal work, so again he also performs the universal work as his conscious object; the whole becomes, as a whole, his own work, for which he sacrifices himself and precisely in so doing receives back from it his own self. (Hegel, 1977, p. 213)

There are two things to observe here. First, the negation of the self through one's labor and the receiving back of the self via the whole, the other. In this process, consciousness takes on new forms and "each new shape it adopts requires that consciousness forego the certainty of itself that its previous shape gave" (Rae, 2012, p. 29). Second, in serving the whole, part of one's labor becomes "fixed labor," labor that was mechanical and specialized to serve the needs of others. This, for Marx, is what makes Hegel's focus on the positive side of labor problematic. From fixed labor man creates surplus, which now feeds back into the dialectic of possession. For, who owns this surplus? It is this surplus, this commodity, through which man sees the other, the whole, but from which he is simultaneously alienated.

As Rae (2012) observes, alienation captures two German words translated as estrangement and externalization. It is the latter understanding—"the process whereby consciousness externalizes itself in object form and, through this objectification, develops a better understanding of itself" (Rae, p. 31)—that is primarily taken up by Marx. The difference between Marx and Hegel here is that, for Hegel, even as economic structures control the worker, they are nonetheless his product as well (Gouldner, 1980). Thus, we have Hegel's contention that this was simply the fate of man. Marx, however, rejects this. As Gouldner argues, "Marx no longer regards alienation as a universal human phenomenon, but links it to the mode of production, in general, and to the property system of capitalism, in particular" (p. 180). The central concern for Marx is, then, to understand labor and its creation of alienating social conditions not as fate but as born of particular historical conditions. Here Marx focuses on the negative impact of labor.

The relationship for Marx—and not, initially, unlike Hegel—is between one's labor and the product of that labor which will have some kind of value, use value or exchange value, because of the labor now embodied in its object. As Marx (1964) puts it, "…this realization of labor appears as a loss of realization for the workers; objectification as loss of the object and bondage to it; appropriation as estrangement, as alienation" (p. 108). The bondage to the object from which one is now alienated is related to Marx's commodity fetishism. That is, man is bonded to the thing because it is now through it, through the commodity, that he knows and is known by the other. As Marx puts it,

> The mysterious character of the commodity-form consists therefore simply in the fact that the commodity reflects the social characteristics of men's own labour as objective characteristics of the products of labour themselves, as the socio-natural

properties of these things. Hence it also reflects the social relation of the producers to the sum total of labour as a social relation between objects, a relation which exists apart from and outside the producers. (Marx, 1977, pp. 164–165)

The fetishized commodity is objectively received as having intrinsic value, thus obscuring the real source of its value, human labor, as well as the exploitative relationship between the laborer and the capitalist. In this process, consciousness no longer recognizes itself in the object. It is here that one form of alienation, externalization, leads to the other form, estrangement: "a process or state where consciousness is separated from, at least, one of the aspects that are required for consciousness to fully understand itself" (Rae, p. 31).

Importantly, Marx understands alienation beyond the relationship between the laborer and her products, identifying three other forms: alienation from the act of production, from the species essence, and from man from man. For Marx (1964), the product is "but the summary of the activity" (p. 110). Furthermore, the activity, as Hegel's fixed labor, is also coerced labor belonging, ultimately, to someone else. It is "not the satisfaction of a need; it is merely a means to satisfy needs external to it" (Marx, 1964, p. 111). As such, and as regards estrangement from the species, estranged labor reverses the role of the conscious being as progenitor of free activity. In this reversal, her essential being turns toward existence and as a means of survival. Such unfree activity is not conscious life activity, that which makes humans a species being. Stripped of their species essence, relationships among people can only be viewed "in accordance with the standard and the relationship in which man finds himself as a worker" (p. 115).

But, it is not just the worker who is captured here. For Hegel, the master ultimately becomes the bondsman or slave to the extent that the former is dependent upon the latter. This, of course, is a line of thinking taken up by Freire regarding oppressor and oppressed. Such lack of freedom for all is taken up by Marx and Engels in the *German Ideology*, as they note, "In the social production of their lives men enter into definite, necessary relations that are independent of their will" (Gouldner, 1980, p. 190).

The difference on this last point between Marx and Hegel is that, for Hegel, in what for Marx is a dialectical reversal, man creates the material conditions that are inescapable. For, contrarily for Marx, it is the material conditions that create man's consciousness, enslaving him thereby. Thus, Marx (1977) points out,

> My dialectic method is, in its foundations, not only different from the Hegelian, but exactly the opposite to it. For Hegel, the process of thinking, which he even transforms into an independent subject, under the name of "the Idea," is the creator of the real world, and the real world is only the external appearance of the idea. With me the reverse is true: the ideal is nothing but the material world reflected in the mind of man, and translated into forms of thought. (p. 102)

That said, as noted previously, it is not clear that Hegel is quite so ahistorical. If the thing that mediates the relationship between master and bondsman is land, it is land that holds the bondsman in subjection. But this "is because of the feudal arrangements per se, and it is the contradiction inherent in feudalism that creates an opening for the bondsman to escape his servitude (Cole, 2005, p. 594). Regardless the particularities of this debate, it is clear that material conditions matter and it is this that grounds Marx's analysis as history takes us from feudalism to capitalism.

Just as the surplus created through labor continued the dialectic of possession in Hegelian thought, it is now surplus labor captured in the phantasm of "capital" by the capitalist that continues it in Marxist thought. Further, it is the now even more exaggerated relation between commodities, the products of one's increasingly fixed labor, that drives alienation. To understand this, Marx shifts his analysis to the relationship between the mode of production *and* the relations of production. In this relationship, the worker is forced to sell his own labor as any other commodity, to the highest bidder, which, within capitalist exploitation, means the highest low bid necessary to profit enhancement for the capitalist, which entails maintenance of the precariat.

Critical Theory

It is commonly recognized that critical pedagogy has its origin in the tradition of critical theory as articulated by members of The Frankfurt School, the *Institut für Sozialforschung*, directed by Max Horkheimer. Horkheimer (1972) develops his notion of critical theory against traditional theory, and, later, with Theodore Adorno (1979), he develops a critique of the instrumentalization of reason as a manifestation of how power functions. This marked a distancing from orthodox Marxism. As Landmann (cited in Tarr, 1977) argues, elements of orthodox Marxist doctrine—historical and dialectical materialism, base and superstructure, economic determinism, a critique of capitalism and class struggle—did not become dominant component parts of critical theory. So an important point of this chapter is to suggest that just as critical theory moved away from these crucial elements so has critical pedagogy more contemporarily. Importantly, however, capitalism is not the only form of domination. Elements of technocracy and bureaucracy also function as forms of domination and the Frankfurt school looked for structural interconnections among such elements.

The distancing from orthodox Marxism by Adorno and Horkheimer is also revealed in their critique of the regimentation of rationality through commodity exchange and toward a critique of instrumental reason (Wellmer, 2014). Of course, Adorno and Horkheimer's take on reason is criticized by Habermas as being far too deterministic and, thus, becoming self-contradictory in their own performances of critique. I, too, depart from Adorno and Horkheimer's more pessimistic view of reason, while cleaving to the idea that common sense and the reason that informs it is, to some degree, preformed mainly through the irrationality of societal structure (capitalism) as Horkheimer had argued earlier.

As regards critical and traditional theory, Horkheimer rejects the mechanical and specialized empiricism of the latter. This is not to suggest that Horkheimer rejected empiricism. Nevertheless, theory construction had become essentially a project of a technical, mathematical logic disconnected from the broader social context and processes. As such, scientists in specialized fields could not lay claim, even as they seemed to operate from such an assumption, to an independent, suprasocial, self-sufficient knowledge which, in the end, is instead "incorporated into the apparatus of society" (Horkheimer, 1972, p. 196). Thus, such scientism served only to fix problems within the existing structure, not to problematize and transform that structure as was the call of critical theory. To wit, if

> The theoretician and his specific object [the proletariat] are seen as forming a dynamic unity with the oppressed class, so that his presentation of societal contradictions is not merely an expression of the concrete historical situation but also a force within it to stimulate change, then his real function emerges. (Horkheimer, 1972, p. 215)

In other words, it is society itself that must be the real object toward the pursuit of some level of equality of condition.

Even as Horkheimer refrains from citing Marx as much as one might expect, Marxism, especially the materialism thereof, is clearly his theoretical orientation. As Tarr (1977) observes, Horkheimer "hoped to salvage the philosophical-theoretical heritage of a humanist Marxism ..." (p. 25). Similarly, Adorno, while suspicious of the more economically deterministic aspects of Marxist thought, stresses Marx's understanding of capitalism, especially the extent to which exchange value determines worth. Thus, both Horkheimer and Adorno employ basic Marxist concepts such as the exchange of commodities—with which a critical theory of society begins for Horkheimer (1972) and which has a totalizing effect on society for Adorno (1973).

Building on this Marxian orientation, Horkheimer makes clear at the outset that the enterprise of the Institute was to engage in studies that seek to understand the material realities of human existence and to alleviate suffering. As he put it in his inaugural address to the Institute, the ultimate aim of social philosophy

> is the philosophical interpretation of *the vicissitudes of human fate*—the fate of humans not as mere individuals, however, but as members of a community. It is thus above all concerned with phenomena that can only be understood in the context of human social life: with the state, law, economy, religion—in short, *with the entire material and intellectual culture of humanity*. (Horkheimer, 1993, p. 1, italics added)

We see Horkheimer's materialism even more directly with his identification of *the* question in discussions concerning society which regards "the connection between the economic life of society, the psychological development of individuals, and the changes in the realm of culture..." (cited in Stirk, 1992, p. 71). This concern also highlights the interdisciplinary research Horkheimer envisioned—as an antidote to the hyperspecialization he saw in the sciences generally. Such interdisciplinarity would be required because not everything traces back to the economy as material being. Indeed, such a claim represented simply vulgar Marxism for Horkheimer.

While critical theory went through various phases and revisions (Tarr, 1977; Wellmer, 2014), its overarching purpose remained the same: "the abolition of social injustice" (Horkeimer, 1972, p. 242). To this point, Michael Landmann (1977) describes critical theory as follows:

> For critical theory, both self-fulfillment and the happiness of the individual depend on the conditions of the whole societal environment. The individual can only achieve self-fulfillment in a society that is liberated from wants and from the oppression of man by man, that is, in a society in which conditions for a dignified human existence are established. (p. vii)

This certainly captures the Liberal principle of flourishing, both in its individual and collective sense as well as other Liberal principles referred to in the previous chapter. And, Horkheimer (1993) reveals these further in his thinking, noting that "each member [of civil society] is his or her own end" (read: autonomous), "but except in contact with others, they cannot attain the whole compass of their ends" (p. 3). Nevertheless, given the necessity of such contact, one must also consider the welfare of others. More strongly, for Horkheimer, individual well-being and happiness is dependent upon the welfare of others. Capitalism, instead, forces people to focus on their individual survival.

Critical Pedagogy

Critical pedagogy promotes education as a mechanism for the transformation of society, the promotion of social justice, emancipation, anti-oppression, etc. As an example, we might consider Aliakbari and Faraji's (2011) description of critical pedagogy: "Through problem posing education and questioning the problematic issues in learners' lives, students learn to think critically and develop a critical consciousness which help them to improve their life conditions and to take necessary actions to build a more just and equitable society" (p. 77). Paolo Freire contrasts this problem posing or "problematizing" approach to a problem-solving approach which would be akin to the mechanistic methodologies criticized by critical theorists. As critical theory "opposes regimentation of the intellect" (Landmann, p. viii), critical pedagogy becomes the instrument of this opposition by working toward a change in consciousness or what Freire termed conscientization.

In working with his adult students in his literacy program, Freire (1976) drew on the vocabulary universe of the students, especially those lexical items that identified the experiential. Freire also relied on rich images that depicted not only the vocabulary but also the cultural experience to which the word(s) attached. The examples below illustrate Freire's approach. These specific examples (from Freire, 1973) were used in "culture circles" in which students expressed in their own words in "dialogue" with each other and the "teacher" (note that Freire rejected the teacher–student binary) their understanding of how their world came to be. Both of the illustrations provide depictions to stimulate such dialogue. The ultimate goal in this approach was for students to understand themselves as subjects in their own history, culture, and future—working toward integration within present society. Here Freire distinguishes between the integrated and the adaptive person. The former "results from the capacity to adapt oneself to reality plus the critical capacity to make choices and to transform that reality," whereas the latter represents the extent to which "man loses his ability to make choices and is subjected to the choices of others" (Freire, 1973, p. 4). The integrated person, then, is subject, whereas the adapted person is object.

Reading nature and culture.

Source: Freire, 1987, pp. 66 and 62, respectively

From the illustrations above, students come to understand themselves as subjects as they come to understand the difference between nature and culture. Whereas the birds in the illustration on the left are of nature, the feather in the man's hair is culture, even as it, too, is from nature. The point is that the transformation of nature and the creation of culture can only be legitimately accomplished by a subject. Similarly, in the illustration on the right, nature (water) was made the object of man's knowledge through work in the construction of the well. In this case, the extent of the cultural and societal transformation may have been enormous. How far had the community had to carry water before the well? How much time in their daily lives did the well free up for other purposes?

Such examples illustrate the deep connection back to Hegel. Freire's process leads essentially to the sublation of the object and the subject. For it is Hegel's slave who, through his labor, asserts his self over the natural world, achieving his own self-consciousness or, more critically for Freire, his conscientization. In other words, conscientization, even as a particular kind of consciousness of power relations, remains a Hegelian phenomenological development of consciousness. For "by coming to see that it has created its objective reality, consciousness will recognize itself in its objective world and so will no longer see its objective world as something simply alien to itself" (Rae, 2012, p. 33). This dialectic of self-consciousness is, as Duquette (n.d.) points out,

> inherent in the very structure of freedom, and is the defining feature of Spirit (*Geist*). The full actualization of Spirit in the human community requires the progressive development of individuality which effectively begins with the realization in self-consciousness of the "truth of self-certainty" and culminates in the shape of a shared common life in an integrated community of love and Reason …. (para. 19)

I should note here the important inclusion of Liberal individualism *alongside* community. Such an understanding precludes the kind of hyper-individualism promoted through neoliberalism. Also, I would add to Duquette's observation by interpreting "integrated" here through Freire. In this way, the community is also subject, providing a sense of the collective autonomy necessary to both criticality and flourishing.

In these examples, we also begin to see the necessary connection for Freire between reflection and action: praxis. This is not just about the quotidian (hunting, obtaining water) but also about reading the political world. This requires not just generic reflection, but reflection through theory that is then connected to action and the production of ways of knowing that challenge relations of oppression. After all, as Goulet observes in his introduction to Freire's (1973) *Education for Critical Consciousness*, one of the goals of literacy was for the oppressed to "perceive their own illiteracy as the cultural artifact of those who would oppress them" (p. viii). Literacy becomes a much broader notion in this sense such that "Man must be made to see the relationship between his activities and what is achieved thereby, between his particular existence and the general life of society, between his everyday projects and the great ideas which he acknowledges" (Horkheimer, 1972, p. 265). Again, the Hegelian themes of self-consciousness, the sublation of the lord/bondsman (oppressed/oppressor for Freire), and a shared common life permeate conscientization.

The Uncritical Role of Schools

The problem is that conscientization has never been an overriding or even important concern of schooling. In terms of the study of schooling more generally, critical pedagogues "examine schools in their historical context and as part of the existing social and political fabric that characterizes the dominant society" (Duncan-Andrade & Morrell, 2008, p. 23). Historically, schools have developed for a number of reasons, chief among them is to act as sorting mechanisms (Abdulkadiroglu, Che, & Yasuda, 2011; Abdulkadiroglu & Sonmez, 2003). Thus, it is understandable that a primary aspect of the existing social and political fabric is economic, leading, in neoliberal fashion, to management-type pedagogies, reductive accountability schemes, the deskilling of teachers, the quest for market-driven excellence, and a reversal of the ideal that "schooling for self and social empowerment is ethically prior to mastery of technical skills, which are primarily tied to the logic of the marketplace" (McLaren, 1989, p. 188).[3] As alluded to in the introduction with the example of Sweden's entrepreneurial purpose for schools, from a Marxian standpoint, the capitalist state does not invest in education from altruism; it invests in the development of human capital. A human's being is for capital development, eclipsing the human being.

This eclipse grotesquely extends all the way down to the most vulnerable people (now laborers) in school, preschoolers. Consider a report provided by the Standards and Testing Agency in the UK which refers to the necessity of testing four-year-old children to obtain a "baseline":

> The purpose of the reception of the baseline is to support the accountability framework and help assess school effectiveness by providing a score for each child at the start of reception which reflects their attainment against a pre-determined content domain and which will be used as the basis for an accountability measure of the relative progress of a cohort of children through primary school. (cited in Boxley, p. 141)

This, of course, is often sold as being able to determine the "value added." The value-added movement feeds into the process of constructing children as commodities. Recall the definition of value added noted in the introduction: the enhancement a company gives its product or service before offering the product to customers. Such a corporate notion should be, but is unfortunately not, taken as gobbledygook when applied to education. As Gene v Glass (2012) observes, "[value-added assessments] act as though the statistical equating on achievement tests (as fallible as it is) of groups of students has held all influences constant (*ceteris paribus*), and hence the gain score is valid and fair as a measure of the contribution to learning of a teacher or a school. It is not, and never will be" (para. 8).

Despite Glass' stern warning, the notion of value added, and other such corporate ideas in education, speaks to the observation in the previous chapter regarding the idea of positive freedom as co-opted by neoliberalism. In that particular idea, the conditions of the market must be created. Given this, critical pedagogues must also see neoliberal schooling as a form of cultural politics since its primary goal is to introduce students to and adapt them to the market order and the concomitant social relations of production. In such social relations, as just noted, one's being is altered and people relate to each other in terms of their productive capacity.

Challenging this requires a change of consciousness through an engagement with emancipatory reason, a form of reason antithetical to the instrumental form of reason required of neoliberalism. Instrumental rationality, informed by the irrationality of capitalism, seeks to uncover means to ends. It does not question the ends. It is about solving problems within the governing social order of neoliberalism, as opposed to problematizing that very order toward more just ends. This latter, then, is emancipatory reason: To wit, "For men to overcome their state of massification, they must be enabled to reflect about that very condition" (Freire, 1973, p. 20). Nevertheless, as part of the current social and political fabric, schools are less about reflection and more about fixity.

(Un)Fixing Education with Critical Pedagogy?

Most educationists who recognize the nefarious effects of neoliberalism on schools and their "academic" outcomes would probably identify critical pedagogy as a now long-standing attempt to unfix schooling. Again, recognizing multiple forms of neoliberalism in different contexts and times, the line that seems to run through is that schools function to legitimize capitalist systems and social relations. The development of a sorting machine model of public education in the early 20th century, for example, certainly fits this more contemporary explanation of neoliberalism. The sorting machine model was accompanied and driven by intelligence testing and what we now refer to as human capital theory (Spring, 2017). Even as that model was ostensibly meant to overcome the deleterious effects of the educational free market and promote equal educational opportunity (and here in conjunction with the previous argument, note the appeal to the basic Liberal principle of equality), the design was a legitimation of a classed model of education.

So where does critical pedagogy stand contemporarily in relation to its critical Marxian roots? Many treatments of critical pedagogy simply ignore or understate the theoretical importance of materialism. As Joan Wink (2011) observes in her very useful and influential book, now in its fourth edition, conscientization "means that we have voice and the courage to question ourselves and the role we are playing in maintaining educational processes that we do not value" (p. 57). Nevertheless, the extent to which critical pedagogues themselves employ this voice in the way that Wink suggests, especially as it would challenge the material realities within schools, is questionable.

For example, in an article on using the Convention on the Rights of Children as a curricular source for transformational education, Christensen, Pendergrass, and Whetstone (2016) explicitly exemplify a tension we see between critical pedagogy and the material conditions of schools. On the one hand, they identify a project of having students read the Convention and understand the rights they have but probably do not often enjoy, especially in schools. This seems soundly "critical," promoting the skills of analysis representative of the purposes of critical pedagogy. On the other hand, even as they want teachers to recognize "that there are [these] broader issues to achieve," "a transformative teacher *does not neglect accountability or standards-based programs.*" After all, teachers must "accomplish standards and improve standardized test scores" (p. 180, emphasis added). In other words, their once critical project gets directed toward technocratic goals and processes because they overlook the space of their practice. They overlook their own feudal context which now also derives from property, the property, or, perhaps more accurately, the commodity of test scores.

To some degree this may be because most classroom applications of critical pedagogy are focused on, as critical pedagogy requires, real-world problems that tend to be beyond the school walls. Such activities rarely seek to problematize the material realities within the school or the power relationships therein, which might disturb the organizational sanctity. A glaring example of this is provided (unintentionally) in an article on the integration of critical pedagogy in an EFL teacher education classroom (Alvarez, Calvete, & Sarasa, 2012). The authors use the movie Slumdog Millionaire and Salmon Rushdie's story "The free radio" to engage students critically. Certainly, the students in this study do so. To wit, the authors point out that "Then, [student 1] calls upon Pedagogy of the Oppressed (Freire, 2006) to reflect on domination and its enabling conditions: 'poor people are left without any possibilities of change as they are not educated, and thus cannot think critically about the Government's abuses…they have no other choice but to accept oppression'" (p. 64). Of course, I cannot say that it never happened in the classrooms of the authors of this article, but I am nevertheless left to wonder if the students ever considered their own oppression dictated by the worldwide hegemony of English. The authors rightly observe that "Language is indeed a privileged means of symbolic domination: control, status, authority, and prominence are all enforced by language" (p. 67). But by "language," they do not refer to "a language" but to "interesting language features." For example, their analysis of one participant's response is: "First, the thematic structure chosen for the initial sentence indicates that the writer's concern was to contrast power relations before and after decolonization, as shown by the discourse marker 'however'" (p. 65). The point is that the exercise in no way troubles the material conditions of the EFL classroom itself. As such, these oppressive conditions go unnoticed, unchallenged, becoming common sense, the common sense being that one should know English. For what? Because English becomes a commodity (not in an orthodox Marxist sense) but something that purportedly provides some sort of value nonetheless.[4] In short, the classroom exercise challenges neoliberal oppression while the classroom and nature of the class reinscribe it.

Similar to Christensen et al. (2016), Schiller (2016) uses the Universal Declaration of Human Rights in Human Rights Education (HRE), an approach to which "critical pedagogy provides a powerful complement" (p. 187). Schiller describes teachers who use a HRE approach in their teaching; she also describes the school. In both, we again see the tension between the material reality of the neoliberal and the critical. First, the school in question maintains a college preparatory focus. This, of course, complements the standard of college and career readiness and the economistic neoliberal baggage that that discourse entails as it focuses on the creation of human capital. Second, the school is an English-only school that, from the description, utilizes a form of structured English immersion. Problematically, then, the school instructional model (immersion) ignores linguistic human rights (Skutnabb-Kangas, Phillipson, & Rannut, 1995) even as teachers employ a human rights discourse in their teaching.[5] But, more germane to my point is the idea that English is the language of economic access, and such a "deficit" must be overcome. Finally, Schiller rightly raises the problem of "seeing education beyond simple content standards for schools to be transformational" even as she problematically supports the alignment of HRE with common core standards. Observing the economic emphasis in the common core standards and its fixation on college and career readiness, Heybach and Sheffield (2014) posit, rightly I think, that "The move to Common Core standards follows a decade of educational policy that seeks to dismantle the traditional understanding of public schooling in America, and replace it once and for all with a privatized system that can overtly be tied to the conflationary economic agenda of advanced capitalism" (p. 77). Of course, educators might agree that all students should achieve a certain level of education—something along the lines of Amy Gutmann's (1987) "democratic threshold" perhaps. Such fixes are easily caught up in the centrifugal force of conservative modernization, becoming part of fixity.

Refining Hegel for Critical Pedagogy

Returning to Wink's earlier observation that we must question ourselves and the role we are playing in maintaining educational processes that we do not value, as these examples above illustrate we do, she does not make clear why we maintain such processes in the first place. To do so requires understanding the power of the material conditions of schools. Given this, it is problematic that in Wink's popular text Marx features over a mere two pages. Further, even as Wink is careful to indicate the difference between Marx's dialectic and Hegelian rationalism, the explicit notion of materialism is left unnamed—an unfortunate oversight for someone who emphasizes naming in her work. (Wink's mantra is "to name, to critically reflect, to act.") On the one hand, I do not want to overstate a concern here. Wink observes that Marx "was attracted to the idea of oppositional historical forces, but Marx [unlike Hegel] did not think of this as simply a theoretical construct to muse on when solving philosophical problems. Rather he saw these opposing ideas as real" (p. 113). This "real," as I will interpret Wink, consists of capitalist social relations and the material conditions thereof. On the other hand, there is a legitimate concern about the rendering of Hegel that this claim entails.

Hegel was, of course, influential as an idealist, albeit in a much more complicated way than Wink suggests. For him the mind and the world follow the same rational principles. Thus, self-consciousness is about finding oneself within that world through the process of alienation. Also, recall that self-consciousness takes different shapes and is a matter of degree as man progresses toward its attainment. Nevertheless, it seems to be that Hegel's legacy remains that of the Idea, despite the fact that, as Lenin reminds of the discussion above, "in this most idealistic of Hegel's works [*Logic*] there is the least idealism and the most materialism" (Anderson, 1995, p. 96).

This legacy owes, in part, to a group of left Hegelians, often referred to as the "Young Hegelians," who take up Hegel's work after his death. For them, certain illusions prevented the development of self-consciousness and, ultimately then, freedom. Chief among these illusions was religion which, for Hegel, went hand in hand with philosophy through which religion presented its truths. Contrarily for the Young Hegelians, religion had to be undone by philosophy and reason. Initially a Young Hegelian himself, Marx came to the conclusion that a rational critique of religion toward the Idea of society (which was the subject) would be insufficient to bring about freedom. Indeed, the subject for Marx was man, and the source of his unfree state would be found in the economy. Critiquing the Young Hegelians, Marx argued that "It has not occurred to any one of these philosophers to inquire into the connection of German philosophy with German reality, the relation of their criticism to their own material surroundings" (Marx & Engels, 1947, p. 87). By ignoring the real conditions of men, the Young Hegelians attributed the "chains" of men to their own consciousness. Thus, they "put to men the moral postulate of exchanging their present consciousness for human, critical or egoistic consciousness, and thus of removing their limitations" (Marx & Engles, p. 86). But, it is important to reassert the materialism in Hegel. The kind of rationalism that Wink attributes to Hegel is the very source of critique Marx had of the Young Hegelians.

Returning back to Wink's understanding of Hegel, my contention is that doing critical pedagogy seems mostly to have boiled down to a traditional and uncritical Hegelian rationalism in resolving contradictions and problems posed. Here is one such example of a task in this vein: "Require the evaluation of existing controversies in contemporary society, such as the relative merits of U.S. government spending on atomic weapons versus international health programs."[6] Of course, weighing the relative merits of a controversy (I would say "so-called controversy" as regards this particular example) is a skill that students must acquire, as critical thinking. But critical thinking may not be the same as thinking critically about the structures that make such a debate tenable or even necessary in the first place. Further, what does it mean to rationally weigh the relative merits without experience of what it means to not have access to health care, especially for privileged students? Such examples simply repeat vulgarizations of Hegelian thought: thesis, antithesis, synthesis, something that Wink also repeats. Do we, then, inculcate in students an idea that the mere realization and consideration of such contradictions is self-consciousness? To put it in Hegelian terms, is it, then, the end of their history? The dialectic of self-consciousness in such an approach is necessary but grossly insufficient.

This becomes even more problematic when Wink conflates Hegel and Socrates. As Wink puts it, "When Hegel enters a transformational classroom, the students peel the onion with each further bit of inquiry" (p. 95). Peeling the onion is when "The facilitator/teacher in a Socratic dialogue in the classroom encourages each student to share his/her point of view on an issue and to create a persuasive argument in a class discussion. Effective Socratic dialogues have a dialectical approach" (p. 95). For Hegel, however, such a mechanical approach can be applied to any thesis, an arbitrary project that he rejected. Instead, the dialectic was, as Hegel pointed out, part of "everything true in general" (cited in Maybee, 2016). Here we must also keep in mind Hegel's (and Marx') materialism wherein the dialectic process is about realizing consciousness through experience, an embodied dialectic. What, then, is the experience in the Socratic dialogue? I would argue that it is not just productive but simultaneously reductive and, therefore, reproductive of the status quo.

Critical pedagogues must provide students exposure to different material conditions and experiences that lead to a different consciousness, conscientization. This said, critical pedagogues must also be cognizant of what might be referred to as negative materialism—when the material conditions and experiences thereof become actively reproductive or reproductive through benign neglect. Halting students' growth at "weighing the relative merits" is an example of the latter and the Texas curriculum an example of the former.

As another example, consider the materiality in the critical—come managerial—pedagogy apparent in one of the activities, a "dialogue journal," Wink describes. In this activity, students are asked to

- o choose any portion of the text and read it silently;
- o write privately in their journal their reactions to the passage;
- o share the passage from the text and her written reflections with another student. (Wink, p. 156)

A similar activity is "pair share," wherein one student from a pair explains a portion of some text to the other student. The text is discussed by the two partners and then shared and discussed with the rest of the class. For Wink, these exercises are "transformational." Of course, more context of the classroom, the text, previous experiences, etc., are necessary to make any real judgment in this regard. However, on the face of it, these activities are not necessarily transformational in any critical sense of the term. The basic skills that students get from activities (the ability to summarize, formulate questions, etc.) are invaluable. But are these not, then, reflective of just more school stuff? These experiences may be more democratic in some ways than traditional didactic teaching and students were relieved to not have to present to the whole group and enjoyed the reflective time, as Wink reports. But, again, the material space of school simply calls such exercises into being as more school stuff, and technocratically and reproductively so.

In fact, prima facie, they aren't even much about dialogue, at least not in the Socratic sense, until the teacher enters and guides the dialogue, which is not suggested in these exercises. Nevertheless, such activities are often referenced when a teacher is asked what they do in terms of critical pedagogy. To the extent that the activities might involve a text that poses some sort of problem to be resolved, then we are back to the critiques of rationalism. This said, I do not want to suggest that such activities are not valuable—a point to which I return in subsequent chapters. My concern is the extent to which talking, dialogue, and rationalism are practiced as being forms of critical pedagogy in and of themselves.

Conclusion

Giroux and Giroux (2006) discuss "the promise of critical pedagogy." Certainly, critical pedagogy provides the conceptual coordinates (hegemony, ideology, privilege, etc.) to engage a language of both critique and possibility, thus serving as "an ethical referent and a call to action for educators" (Giroux & Giroux, 2006, p. 30). In this optimistic sense, schooling perhaps becomes a site for radical democratic engagement, the production of an active and engaged citizenry that deliberates on social issues in the hope of a newly possible future. Obviously, my rendition of the reproductive power of neoliberal institutions (such as today's schools) does not immediately share this optimism. While I value critical pedagogy in its promise to transform both education and society toward critical democracy, it is simply failing to take on a fundamental charge to challenge the material conditions of schools and their reproductive capacity. In so doing, the labors to which students are put are unlikely to work toward self-consciousness and certainly not conscientization.

Critical pedagogy can certainly engage the material circumstance of school but tends not to as practiced. This is, in part, because critical pedagogy has become uncritical, becoming an error of commission as it fixes itself, the congeries of techniques of group work, rational and rationalized problem-solving and merit-weighing, and vulgar constructivism being caught in the centrifugal force of conservative modernization. To avoid this, critical pedagogues must, first, remember and sharpen the Marxist edge with which the mold of critical pedagogy was originally cut.

Otherwise, practitioners of uncritical pedagogy promote the illusion of autonomy within the governing rationality. Apropos to this, recall the earlier example that transformative educators cannot abandon accountability or standardized test scores. They must increase standardized test scores. It is one thing to suggest that increased standardized test scores might be an outcome of critical pedagogy, which is likely. It is another thing to suggest that critical pedagogues must actively seek to increase such scores, centering that as a goal in the process. In other words, the suggestion, as I see it, is that critical pedagogues must work within the governing rationality. This is oxymoronic.

The other techniques identified, especially to the extent that they reify rationalism, are similarly problematic in the creation of the illusion of autonomy. For the governing rationality and the material space of schools simply overwhelm these techniques even if and when they are critically oriented. Consider students engaged in the dialogue journal or pair share activity. Even if they are reading and discussing a real problem—let's say something like capitalist exploitation of children through the promotion of unhealthy choices—what surrounds them in school? Well, even as the discussion in this scenario might turn to the increase of cases of serious type II diabetes among children and corporate complicity therein, a short distance down the hallway from this critical discussion is a soda machine. It probably only sells Coke or Pepsi products, never both, due to exploitative, exclusive soda contracts. But the immediate point here is that having completed a critical analysis of the dominant capitalist ideology behind the appearance of myriad soda machines in their school hallways, for example, students can immediately purchase their soda while switching classes. They remain a *Captive Audience*. In this case, their captivity provides them the illusion of autonomy as they choose their soda of their own free will, even more free as they now understand the health dangers and their own exploitation and their behavior becomes "reasoned." In short, the ideal dialectic gets caught in the material web.

Perhaps such understanding is all we can expect of autonomy and so-called free will: (1) That they always involve some sort of manipulation—after all we are not born desiring soda and (2) that we can still make informed choices, even if they are inadvisable ones. Dahlbeck (2017) argues from a Spinozan perspective that "we are moved to act not by a special faculty but by ordinary affects that can transform us in a positive or negative direction" (p. 737). The positive direction in this example is that students now at least understand why and how their choice and subsequent action is unhealthy and can then choose to make smarter choices in the long run, for example, limiting their intake of unhealthy products. More importantly, however, Dahlbeck's point must be directed toward the relational and flourishing in which the positive direction is not just to be true to oneself and one's own flourishing but also true to others and their flourishing. This requires understanding the manipulation that is involved in their purchase, how that is generated by prior manipulations, and how this larger network affects how we relate to one another and create inequality and hierarchies that, in turn, differentially affect different groups of people.

Certainly critical pedagogues recognize the need for schools to provide an empowering education (Shor, 1992) and to promote the democratic ideal of education through a discourse of counter-hegemonic practices (Giroux, 1988) that edges toward such understanding. Furthermore, they recognize that such visions are "in direct opposition to many entrenched educational methods" (Hinchey, 2004, p. 121). The problem is that most critical pedagogues, relying on Freire, tend to rely too facilely on his distinction between problem-posing and banking pedagogy. Problem-posing education, even one that is critically oriented toward social justice, remains far too rationalistic, thereby becoming just another task among the many for students to complete. Certainly, there is power in engaging students in questioning their own assumptions, analyzing their lived experiences, challenging the standard curriculum, understanding whose interests are served by that curriculum and myriad other policies in and out of school, and revealing the contradictions between society and value claims of equality, liberty, etc.

Nevertheless, critical pedagogy, even when it reengages its Marxist roots in more critical fashion as opposed to the uncritical fixity which popular practices can reinscribe, cannot alone provide a robust enough experience to counter fully the material effects of schooling. Here, of course, I can be charged with the critique of overdeterminism provided by resistance theorists against reproduction theorists. So, I note, on the one hand, Marxism helps us identify the problem of fixity and why and where education has become fixed (e.g., through the conservatively modern material conditions of schools that are both derivative and reproductive of capitalist social relations and alienation from school labor). Marx also gives us a robust understanding of the material in relation to social change, recognizing change as necessarily orienting from the material base and toward the superstructure. Finally, Marx provides a sense of class solidarity and a notion of the species being necessary to some understanding of collective autonomy. This remains key to human flourishing.

On the other hand, while Marxism importantly vivifies the possibility and helps to reveal the sources of fixity, it is not at all clear that critical pedagogy driven by orthodox Marxism can move us to resistance in the material space of schools, at least not toward a deep resistance that moves students (or teachers) from objects to subjects. Thus, it is important to move beyond strict Marxism and economic determinism by which the subject is always already object. While understanding capitalism, it is necessary to consider not just how the base is material but also how ideology functions toward reproduction through the superstructure. Here I want to contrast the ideological singularity of Marx with the ideological multiplicity of Althusser to consider different and multiple kinds of resistive spaces beyond the possibility provided by Marx. Given Marx's singularity and understanding that ideology functions in multiple ways through conservative modernization, Marx is not as useful in mapping or interrogating ideology as Althusser. Admittedly, many of the examples in this chapter are already more Althusserian than Marxist in that they (e.g., testing) are material representations of ideology. This point sets the motivation of the next chapter.

Notes

1. Tarr (1977) notes, for example, that Horkheimer criticizes Marx on several accounts including Marx's claim of the inevitable historical trend toward freedom. Tarr also points out how, in a period in which the works of Schopenhauer and Marx came together for

Horkheimer, Horkheimer takes a much more conservative tack, misinterpreting Marx in the process. Aronowitz (2002) also observes that Horkheimer never refers to his approach as Marxist.
2. This is not to suggest there are not many other important influences on Marx in this regard. Feuerbach would come immediately to mind to most scholars in this area.
3. Given this, it is strange that Freire himself rarely talked about materialism. As Gibson (2006) points out, "The words *political economy* or *surplus value* received little attention in his works" (p. 196).
4. See Petrovic (forthcoming) for a critique of understanding language as commodity.
5. Perhaps they justify this given the UDHR does not mention language, raising the problem that the UDHR reinforces linguistic oppression. As egregiously, the school operates from the perspective of the long discredited notion of semi-lingualism (MacSwan, 2000; Martin-Jones & Romaine, 1986).
6. Taken from Wikiversity's entry, *Introduction to Critical Pedagogy*, available at https://en.wikiversity.org/wiki/Introduction_to_Critical_Pedagogy.

· 3 ·

CRITICAL PEDAGOGY WITHIN AN IDEOLOGICAL STATE APPARATUS

In this chapter, I draw on the work of Louis Althusser to move a materialist analysis out of the base and into the superstructure. Althusser, in contrast to Marx, provides a robust understanding of ideology (among other instruments of power identified in the superstructure) as material itself and not just feeding back into Marx's material base. Building on Marx, Althusser (2014) asserts, "it is in ideology that people become conscious of the class struggle and fight it out" (p. 155). For Althusser, this fight is wholly material, manifesting within the reproductive practices of the ideological apparati. But, for Althusser, ideology does not sit distinctly outside the base; such lines of demarcation are necessarily blurred. As Althusser writes, "Ideology does not exist in the 'world of ideas' conceived as a 'spiritual world'. Ideology exists in institutions and the practices specific to them.... more precisely: ideology exists *in apparatuses* and the *practices specific to them*" (p. 156, original emphasis). Further, far from existing within the ideal, ideas themselves "have a *mutual existence*" (p. 156, original emphasis). This materialist rendering of not only ideology but also of laws, rules, the courts, schools, and other ideological state apparati (ISAs) opens up new analyses of how societies function and the role that schools play in that functioning. Schools—through their material ideological presentation (their architecture, their epistemic commitments, and their managerial operationalization through schedules, bells, periods, etc.)—and schooling (as pedagogy)—through its drills, detentions, trackings, groupings, competitive grading, etc.—combine to call us into being—not just through the base collectively, but through the superstructure collectively *and* individually. As such, both schools themselves and schooling (as practices) are material and require a material analysis and intervention. *These* material conditions can be engaged and changed and it is here, through Althusser, that critical pedagogy might continue to sharpen its edge.

Patrick Shannon's (2007) critique of scripted reading programs exposes the necessity of the analytical shift from Marx to Althusser. Shannon argues that teachers who tailor their work to particular students, for particular reasons, and in particular contexts enact "resistance to the rationalization of reading education, the consequent reification of reading instruction as commercial programs, and their objective alienation from their work as teachers" (p. 168). For Shannon, such improvisational teachers follow Marx's historical project to secure the conditions of free activity, self-affirmation, spontaneity, and the development of our physical and mental energy. Nevertheless, this analysis, while Marxian, is not Marxist to the extent that the resistance here occurs at the level of the superstructure. In orthodox Marxism, only the base is material. Ideology, within the superstructure, is not. Thus, the material relations of production represented in the base is what determines our consciousness for Marx, not ideology, not other aspects of the superstructure (laws, regulations, etc.) which have no materiality. Importantly, then, Shannon's analysis should be read not only as Marxian but also as Althusserian.

A concern here might be that such engagement at the level of the superstructure becomes just another form of the ideal dialectic, bringing about, at best, a reformist mentality easily appropriated into the normative relations of production without fundamentally changing those relations (held within the base). Althusser (2014) commented on such acritical activities as revolution *"in the weak* sense" that involves only modifications to ISAs and "represented a family class struggle between dominant classes" (p. 150). The near normalization of critical pedagogy *in the weak sense* in teacher education programs is perhaps emblematic of Althusser's claim regarding reform as a facile struggle among groups who already claim a dominant or otherwise privileged position in society. Nevertheless, the point is that Althusser builds on Marx in a way that requires us to continue to pursue an understanding of the way that our material conditions can shape the subject (who, for Marx, is always already subjected). To reiterate, this shaping, for Marx, occurred through the base.

For Althusser, it occurs both through base and superstructure—the latter necessarily including the ISA of school which becomes part of the ideological material. Schooling, of critical, conservative, or other disposition, can never be extracted from material context of the base and, therefore, instantiates the materiality of the superstructure. When schooling is situated thusly, that is, as a material practice, possibilities for critical engagements productively shift and change. In short, what I am suggesting is that critical pedagogy cannot succeed from an orthodox Marxist perspective; it requires this Althusserian shift.

Digging more deeply into the material realities of the move from neoliberalism to fix education introduced in Chapter 1, in this chapter I attempt to dig into ways that neoliberal ideology functions to reinscribe the existing social order through schools, already inherently conservative institutions. Building on an Althusserian reading of materialism, I will try to oppose the "reduction of the real to the concept" (LaClau, 1984, p. 43)—a problem that has hampered critical pedagogy's attempts to activate progressive change through schooling. Before this, a deeper reading of ideology through Althusser is necessary.

Althusser on Ideology

For Althusser, all ideologies are expressed in practices (be they of individuals or elements of the ISA). Althusser writes that ideology exists *"in the practices"* of those individuals involved in production and, as practices, they never reside solely in the area of ideas (p. 156, original emphasis). These practices are, by definition, materially ensconced; there can be no practices in the abstract—indeed, the very notion of abstracted practices might be read as an ideological means for producing docile subjects. Thus it is that ideology is *expressed*, practiced within the very material conditions that make them possible.

In this way, Althusser emphasizes the material orientation of his theory and orients himself within a Marxian lineage that situates power not in the ideal, but in the material formations of the everyday. Unfortunately, more contemporary scholars, particularly in the field of education, have not always attended to the material elements of Althusser's conception of ideology. All too often, "ideology" has become a throwaway term that remains overly generalized and simplistically ambiguous. Therefore, it remains important to revisit Althusser's use of the term, particularly as it applies to subject formation within the ISA of education. Specifically, Althusser (1971) writes, "ideology does not exist *in ideas*" and has no ideal existence (p. 156, original emphasis). Indeed, ideas themselves have a *material existence* that requires a concerted analysis of the material contexts in which ideas manifest. If ideas themselves are material, then surely the practices that extend as logical articulations of ideology are similarly grounded. Thus, the very idea of schooling—what it can/should be and its uses in particular contexts—exists in dialectical relation to the material circumstances through which schooling practices are known and made visible. And yet, it must be noted, it is through this very materiality of ideology that Althusser (2014) finds the ISA as "infinitely more vulnerable" to possibilities for radical change than other formations of the state (p. 153). With this, then, the materiality of schooling plays an essential role in the possibilities for teachers and students to engage critically, as subjects.

Famously, Althusser characterized the ideological formation of subjects as a process of *interpellation*. As Althusser writes, "*all ideology hails or interpellates concrete individuals as concrete subjects*" (p. 190, original emphasis). It is thus a function of ideology to concretize subjection (the process of subject formation), to legitimize select subjects through their manifestation in material contexts (after all, if a subject formation were to simply reside in the ideal, it would not have the power of impacting daily practices of living on the local scale—presenting instead an idea that might not align with daily experience).

Interpellation thus exists as an everyday practice, one Althusser (2014) termed a "terribly material ritual" through which the subject is ideologically formed (p. 191, n. 24). Importantly, interpellation does not occur because of ideology (nor is ideology constructed through hailing practices): "*the existence of ideology and the hailing or interpellation of individuals as subjects are one and the same thing*" (p. 191, original emphasis). Ideology, then, exists as the material relations of interpellation: subjects formed in the concrete contexts in which they are known. As a consequence, any theorization of subject formation, no matter how well-intended, loses its critical import if it begins—and remains—in abstraction. Such abstractions remain inherently reductive, both in their descriptive articulations and in their possibility for imagining radical social change at the ideological level.

Given this, when critics seek to intervene in dominant practices of schooling in the hopes of instigating some element of progressive social change, they must be careful to recognize the materiality of such practices even as they guard against the seduction of abstraction. Indeed, critical engagements that rely on abstraction ensure that "nothing is happening": "when nothing is happening the Ideological State Apparatuses have worked to perfection" (Althusser, 2014, p. 206). The goal, for Althusser, is to intervene in the easy replication of ideological practices, to disrupt the functioning of the ISAs (such as the school) and, thereby, make possible that events happen. It is my continuing concern that critical pedagogy has missed the charge of materialism even as such theorists attempt to theorize interventions in the normative status quo of schooling. In short, critical pedagogues often theorize and, "nothing is happening." What must be done to make possible the event of interruption?

As the most dominant ISA (replacing, for Althusser, the dominance of the Church in contemporary society), schools play an important role in teaching "know-how"—the ideology of common sense that, through its very commonness, maintains the easy function of the ISA and ensures "*subjection to the dominant ideology*, or else the 'practice' of it" (p. 52, original emphasis). These activities remain intimately tied to the material circumstances through which they play out. Recognize, for example, the easy replication of the geography of schools and classrooms across time and space—regimented spaces that, most often, situate teachers in the front (as manager) and students in rows or groups (some say, "pods") of desks, all engaged in the practices of schooling.

Admittedly, this claim is similar to the one made by US Secretary of Education Betsy DeVos. As reported, "Does this look familiar?" she tweeted, showing side-by-side stock photos from different eras of children sitting in desks, facing the teacher. "Students lined up in rows. A teacher in front of a blackboard. Sit down; don't talk; eyes up front. Wait for the bell. Walk to the next class. Everything about our lives has moved beyond the industrial era. But American education largely hasn't" (Will, 2018, para. 5). This sentiment echoes similar comments by former Secretary of Education under President Obama, Arne Duncan, who decried the extent to which schools still follow an "industrial-age factory model of education" (US Dept of Education, 2010, para. 22). In response to DeVos, many teachers responded with pictures from their own classrooms that show flexible seating arrangements, group work, and freedom of movement.[1]

Nevertheless, even as the "industrial age," as it tends to be applied to thinking about schools and education, cannot rightly be considered a single, planned, nationally coherent phase (Dorn, 2011), it certainly was the case that, historically, students sat, by and large, in rows in teacher-centered classrooms. Due to a variety of forces such as immigration, urbanization, and child labor laws, increases in school attendance required that "Schools built during the last decades of the 19th century and early decades of the 20th century were therefore largely standardized, utilitarian spaces that were designed to house as many students as possible, maximizing classroom space" (Baker, 2012). Such classroom settings continue to be (re)created across the country day in and day out. Students and teachers walk into these rooms, recognize them without hesitation, and "nothing happens." Thus it is that, for Althusser, schooling has an ideological effect of making normative relations of production "go all by themselves" (p. 201). Furthermore, as they "go," they co-opt their very critique as well as co-opting the identities of students and teachers. In this vein, Symeonidis (2014) points out the effect of the introduction of neoliberal reforms to schooling in Sweden: "New identities have been introduced, such as the consumer, school advertiser and entrepreneur" (p. 35).

Reconsider, for example, the renewed critiques of "factory schools." This long-held progressive mantra has now been taken up by neoliberals. Certainly, underscoring the faults in public education enhances policy initiatives toward "innovation" driven by the market. In this way, the complaint about schools as factories becomes a ploy to turn schools into corporations. Such moves are ideologically innovative, and indicative of the adaptable predation of neoliberalism, but certainly not educational innovation. Acevedo (2019) points out, for example, the decimation of public school systems through the entrepreneurialism of for-profit Educational Management Organizations (EMOs) after hurricane Katrina in New Orleans.

Within our contemporary contexts, these key elements of ideology accelerate and disperse into a wide array of contexts and practices, presenting unique challenges to the intrepid criticalist intent on social change (or in transitioning away from schooling where "nothing is happening" to critical education as an "event" that disrupts the easy replication of know-how or the normative status quo). As such, I next consider how ideology manifests within the context of conservative modernization.

How Ideology Functions in Conservative Modernization

Ideology manifests in a number of ways including through legitimation, dissimulation, unification, fragmentation, and reification (Thompson, 1990). All of these are relatable to neoliberalism specifically or the various components of conservative modernization more generally. Legitimation, for example, creates the impression or belief that unequal power relations are not only legitimate but also in everybody's interest. Thus, the fairness of the distribution of wealth in capitalism is assumed as legitimate in spite of obvious and perverse material differences. Thus it is that change is most often recognized on the individual level (the ability for someone, say, to climb out of the working class and into the comforts of middle-class existence through the timeless values of hard work and determination) over and above change that might happen at the group or class level (that the working poor might achieve a circumstance where basic needs such as housing, healthcare, and education were met, resulting in a flattening of traditional economic hierarchies). Of course, for change to happen beyond the level of the individual, basic principles of capitalism would necessarily be reconstructed operating according to alternative values, in newly constructed material contexts. Paul Willis (1977) famously made this point, writing,

> To the *individual* working class person mobility in this society may mean something. Some working class individuals do 'make it' and any particular individual may hope to be one of them. To the class group at its own proper level, however, mobility means nothing at all. The only true mobility at this level would be the destruction of the whole class society. Thus, we see that it is crucial for those in power that the process of legitimation function efficiently. Further, it must begin early; therefore, schools become uniquely important as ISAs. (p. 128, original emphasis)

In schools, standardized testing is used as a tool of legitimation in the service of hyper-individualism (another fundamental tenet of Liberalism run amuck under neoliberalism). Purportedly fair and neutral assessments lead to the acceptance by students in the socio-academic pecking order (and the concomitant expectations of teachers). In order to alter the normative rationale that makes standardized testing logical (and legitimate) the ideological practices of individualism would need to be delegitimized, shown to produce harmful material contexts for students, teachers, and society alike.

In a similar vein, Stephen Vassallo (2013) provides an interesting analysis of the increasingly influential idea of self-regulated learning. Self-regulated learning teaches students to take responsibility for their own learning, to set goals, to monitor and evaluate their learning and the learning process (in a form of metacognition) (Boekaerts, Pintrich, & Zeidner, 2000), and to activate and sustain cognitions, affects, and behaviors oriented toward learning goals (Zimmerman & Schunk, 2011). But as Vassallo argues it from a Freirean perspective, "teaching students to self-regulate their learning aligns with the neoliberal logic to produce adaptable, self-interested, responsibilized individuals so they can operate within environments that are characterized by choice, competition, and personalized learning" (p. 568). As self-regulated learning increasingly becomes a goal of contemporary education, it not only creates dependency on situational demands and the material conditions of schools, but also is part of such demands. In short, something that seems to be in the best interest of the student and her educational autonomy is co-opted by the extant social order of the school (curricular configurations, testing requirements, grading, and even the physical nature of egg-crate schools). Self-regulated learning reinforces an assumed value of establishing oneself as an individual, responsibly engaging in educational activity. Such practices of individualization are made visible to others through demonstrating one's progress through a series of data points. Thus, "responsibilized" students engage in self-regulated learning as simultaneous acts of seeking out and becoming data points within the neoliberal educational system.[2]

Through dissimulation relations of domination are hidden or obscured or even denied. Here we can look back at the Texas curricular standards which overtly deny alternative accounts of how society functions or could function. Or, we might think of current school practices such as tracking which is said to serve the best interest of students, especially those in lower tracks. Here the relationship to legitimation should also be apparent. This is even as we know that academic tracking in schools has significant negative effects on the academic achievement of students in lower groups (Fogelman, 1983; Kerckhoff, 1986) and, therefore, certainly does nothing to close the achievement gap (Chmielewski, 2014).

Another aspect of dissimulation in regard to the denial of domination is the opaqueness of ideology itself. In other words, the ideological character of ideology does not reveal itself. Ideology functions toward its own denegation. As Althusser proposed, "…it is not their real conditions of existence, their real world, that 'men' represent to themselves in ideology, but above all it is their relation to those conditions of existence which is represented to them there" (p. 64). And the creation of this imaginary is precisely the power of ideology and why the use of the repressive state apparatus—power that functions through violence and force through the military, police, prison and legal system—actually indicates a weak ideological regime. "Much better," as Kavanagh argues, "is a situation in which everyone—from dominant and subordinate class alike—understands and perceives the prevailing system of social relations as fundamentally fair on the whole...and/or as better than any possible alternative, and/or as impossible to change anyway" (p. 308).

The opaqueness of ideology or its self-denegation allows people to insist on their own nonideological position, even as their positions come clearly, quite narrowly, and specifically from the dominant ideology. Boxley (2017) provides a number of cogent examples, provided by policy makers in the UK, of how this manifests. Standing out as one such example is then Secretary of State for Education Michael Gove. In a scheme to restructure schooling along market principles of competition, Gove proclaimed, this "is not about ideology. It's an evidence-based, practical solution built on by successive governments...the new ideologues are the enemies of reform, the ones who put doctrine ahead of pupils' interests" (cited in Boxley, p. 112). Notice, then, how market principles do not come from an ideology; somehow, they simply reflect common sense and only those who disagree come from some ideological space. In this way, policy makers like Gove can be everywhere while pretending to come from nowhere; while those on the left can be nowhere while pretending to come from somewhere. As I pointed out at the end of Chapter 1, understanding the nonideological or nonpolitical insistence from the right as, in fact, political, the left cannot itself make the mistake of a nonpolitical insistence.

Unification serves to create a collective entity that reifies an us/them view of the world, the creation of a real or imagined enemy. In this sense, "we" cannot exist without "them." At the widest level, we might consider the extent to which a primary political purpose of schools is to create what Benedict Anderson (2006) refers to in his theory of nationalism as an "imagined community." The nation "is imagined because the members of even the smallest nation will never know most of their fellow-members, meet them, or even hear of them, yet in the minds of each lives the image of their communion" (p. 6). In the United States especially, patriotic correctness helps to drive such an image. This manifests through the curricular deception of American exceptionalism. For example, most Americans would likely be incensed at the suggestion that it was not the United States that played the most pivotal role in defeating Nazi Germany. Yet, the full historic record may demonstrate this to be the case (Erickson, 1975, 1983; Glantz, 1995). Probably as a result of the cold war, this full record is something that is still not provided.[3] Consider also the "patriotic" daily ritual recital of the pledge of allegiance in schools—a pledge to which the words "under God" were added years after its first publication specifically in order to emphasize the us vs. them world of the Cold War. The function of unification is to deflect attention away from unequal power relationships given that we are all in the same boat, so to speak.

Related to unification is fragmentation, wherein hegemony is achieved by dividing "them." We see this in the ongoing reduction in class solidarity and attacks against unions, given the competition among, mainly, people of color to sell their labor power. While increasingly obvious since the election of Ronald Reagan, this is certainly not a new phenomenon. Consider Booker T. Washington's Atlanta Compromise Speech of 1895 wherein he pits Black laborers against "those of foreign birth," begging whites to "Cast down your bucket where you are." While perhaps pragmatic, it was, nevertheless, predictable given social relations at the time and the "fix" both required and desired by the dominant social order. In the world of schooling, fragmentation manifests in debates around "dumbing down" the curriculum. Here discussion revolves around purportedly declining standards because of certain groups of students, usually poor and of color, unless, of course, they are a part of some imagined "model minority."

In this way, different groups are not just fragmented but in their fragmentation become reified—separated from the myriad economic, political, social, and historical processes from which they emerged as if they simply existed. Reification thus represents unequal social relations as natural or inevitable: biological differences explain gender inequality in pay structures or racial differences in intelligence (consider, for example, Herrnstein and Murray's [1994] repugnant *Bell Curve*). We also see curricular reification in the "great books" movement or things like Hirsch's "cultural literacy" or his graded series "What Your [first, second, third, etc] Grader Needs to Know."

Finally, adding to Thompson's list, it is necessary to consider the role that distraction plays in the functioning of ideology. Here the trivial or inane becomes so important that consent can be manufactured (Herman & Chomsky, 1988). Consider the phenomenal rise of something like fantasy football where clearly intelligent people can recite the statistics of hundreds of players and intricate details of what could make or break a particular player's season. Many of these same people cannot name the current Secretary of State or other major political players or any details of major policy initiatives. In this way, important initiatives such as the Affordable Care Act (aka, Obamacare) can simply be dismissed by the "it's socialist" sound bite.

How Neoliberal Ideology Functions as Violence and Cultural Invasion

Beyond these more typical ways of discussing ideology and how it functions, I build on the critique of neoliberalism from the previous chapter, now explicitly arguing that it is both a form of violence that manifests as cultural invasion (Freire, 1989). Such cultural invasion begets necrophilia (Fromm, 1973) for which unschooling—which I take up in Chapter 4—may be a necessary antidote.[4] From there, I return to the rhetorical device of "fixing," situating necrophilia as a cultural desire to fix what might otherwise be read as fluid systems and processes, a desire that extends from capitalistic values and practices, certainly visible within the field of education. Such desires manufacture both individually known and culturally felt experiences of alienation, which are symptomatic of an imperialist nostalgia that permeates educational policy and daily classroom practices.

The notion of necrophilia is borrowed from Fromm who, in turn, borrows Hans von Hentig's definition: Necrophilia is "the passionate attraction to all that is dead, decayed, putrid, sickly; it is the passion to transform that which is alive into something unalive; to destroy for the sake of destruction; the exclusive interest in all that is purely mechanical. It is the passion to tear apart living structures" (Fromm, 1973, p. 332) and is used here as intended by von Hentig in its characterological sense and beyond the strict biological sense of "aliveness" (although the latter notion too is certainly invoked). A focus on the mechanical reveals important ways in which alleged manifestations of aliveness—alleged through the dominant ideologies of contemporary society, i.e., neoliberalism and neoconservativism—must be problematized, especially as they function in schooling practices and policies to reproduce the social order.

Analysis of existential situations of oppression, argues Freire, reveals that their inception lay in an act of violence—initiated by those in power. Arguably, neoliberalism or, more directly, the policies that derive from a neoliberal ethos should be considered acts of violence. Certainly, acts of enclosure in feudal times (aka, theft)—a form of what Marx called primitive accumulation—were acts of violence against the peasantry, leaving them landless and beholding to the "owners" of now privatized lands to whom to sell their labor power with continued and amplified exploitation.

Through an Althusserian lens, such acts of violence generate from and are supported by the materiality of ideology, that is, the rules, laws, and procedures written by and for capitalists. This is all required to allow accumulation by dispossession to occur. Led by what Peet (2003) calls the "Unholy Trinity" for their ability to destroy local economies, wreak havoc on the environment, and exacerbate poverty and joblessness—the World Trade Organization, the International Monetary Fund, and the World Bank—there might be no better example than the privatization of something so basic to human survival as drinking water. In Chile, for example, the World Bank imposed a loan condition guaranteeing a private French company a 33% profit margin (a little less than what the company was demanding) for providing water services. The privatization of water services has resulted in rising cost (and, of course, profit), declining water quality, and people going without a basic, natural resource: clean water (Shiva, 2001b). Similar examples of profit over people can be found in the privatization of public transportation and public pensions, among many others, driven not only by the specific institutions mentioned, but generally through extant social relations, the neoliberal values that inform them, and the laws designed to uphold them.

As Jean Anyon (2011) points out, "In contrast to investment in traditional production, privatization and accumulation by dispossession do not increase the assets in a society" (p. 87). As a result, accumulation by dispossession presents a doubled violence by first dispossessing the public of what used to be theirs and, by the lack of investment in traditional production, further jeopardizing the individuals' ability to sell their labor power for basic survival, increasingly required by the rising cost of once private goods.

In education, we witness the increased privatization of "public" schools through EMOs. Here I understand privatization to refer to traditional private schools as well as quasi-privatization in the form of EMO-run charter schools. Miron, Horvitz, and Gulosino (2013) report that for-profit EMOs have increased in the United States from 5 to 97 since 1995 and the number of schools they operate has increased from 6 to 840. Despite the promises made by these for-profits, students who attend these schools tend not to do any better than comparison groups. (See, for example, Miron and Applegate's (2000) study of schools run by Edison Schools, Inc.) Under similar choice schemes in Sweden, "Differences between schools have increased and the comparative performance of the country has declined" (Symeonidis, 2014, p. 31). A catalyst for the increase in for-profit EMOs has been the growth in another neoliberal reform model, charter schools. Such choice schemes represent a quasi-privatization of public schools, especially when run by EMOs.

Although they may be improving, we know, for example, that charter schools operated by EMOs are significantly more segregated—and slightly more so under for-profit management—than traditional schools in local public districts along lines of race, class, special needs, and language. We also know that charter schools result in funding losses for traditional public schools. A study by Innovation Ohio (2013), for example, noted a 6.5% loss for public schools in the state of Ohio. Similarly, Bifulco and Reback (2011) estimated a loss in per pupil expenditure in the range of $633 to $1070 across two school districts, Albany and Buffalo, in New York State.

So, here we see an educational parallel to Anyon's point about the lack of investment, intimately tied to the dispossession of public resources that precedes such negative action. We can see how this functions through the example in the most recent charter school legislation to pass in Alabama, Senate Bill 45, which follows a fairly typical model. Under this bill, charter schools receive 100% of federal and state funds and local tax revenue (up to 10 mills). The problem here is that, in the United States, school funds are distributed to districts by variations on a formula dependent on average daily attendance. Thus, since Alabama is not investing more in education, the funds mentioned are not new funds. These are funds that the traditional public school would have received but that now follow the student to the charter school. Since schools in high-poverty areas tend to have lower average daily attendance for a variety of reasons beyond the control of the school, they are susceptible to inadequate funding anyway. Furthermore, since only fourteen US states have progressive funding systems, wherein greater funding is provided to high-poverty school districts (Baker, Sciarra, & Farrie, 2010), any decline in funds is especially problematic for those districts most in need and who serve high-poverty students who simply cost more to educate. This is exacerbated by the fact that EMO-run schools typically serve fewer special needs students and English language learners (Miron, Urschel, Mathis, & Tornquist, 2010). This is, then, a form of adverse selection that requires traditional public schools to do more (serve higher needs students) with less. In short, Alabama's Senate Bill 45 potentially removes public funds from public schools even as it refuses any new investment in the educational sector. Such privatization increases financial stress on those schools with the least capacity to respond—a doubled violence to be sure.

The privatization of public schools raises perennial questions about the loss of public purpose for education, public accountability, and what and whose interests are served. If private corporations run schools, do the educational purposes change accordingly to serve corporate needs as opposed to societal needs and concerns about democracy? The question of democratic schooling is brought into even starker relief once we understand that EMO-run schools are highly segregative (Miron et al., 2010). Are privatized schools accountable to the public writ large, parents of children in the school, or stockholders and other capitalist profiteers? Does profit become the overriding interest and, if so, which children are most profitable? Even as conservatives contemn "government schools," the same questions can be raised about extant public education, which is still largely reproductive of the existing social order as theorized some time ago by Bowles and Gintis (1976), as empirically demonstrated by Anyon (1980) shortly thereafter, and confirmed years later (Bowles & Gintis, 2002a, 2002b). This reproduction occurs through oblique cultural transmission by the school system. Here Bowles and Gintis (2002a) point to a large body of work on the societal transmission of values passed on from generation to generation either vertically (from parents) or obliquely (from others in the prior generation). "The school system," they argue, "is an unusual form of oblique transmission whereby a particular group of people that is often quite unrepresentative of the population of parents [in this case teachers] occupy privileged positions as behavioral models for children" (p. 18). In other words, teachers and, I would add, the structure, policies, and practices in schools socialize students into certain values, even as they may or may not be consistent with parental values. This is largely through the structure of sanctions and rewards that underlies the correspondence principle (Bowles & Gintis, 2002a). Of course, socialization also occurs through the "corporate assault on youth" both in and out of schools (cf. Boyles, 2008). This assault consists of positioning students as consumers, which becomes unethically prior to their development as autonomous individuals. Such depressing circumstances certainly do not occur on their own—they extend from a series of social desires that collude to contain educational processes even as they expand possibilities for economic growth for some.

Necrophilia, Desire, and Fixing Alienation

The corporate takeover of schools, either as a form of primitive accumulation (as exemplified by the incursion of EMOs) or the neoliberal assault on students, is particularly problematic since it inculcates what Freire (1989) calls a possessive consciousness which "tends to transform everything surrounding it into an object of its domination," including people themselves (p. 44). "The more the oppressors control the oppressed," Freire (1989) continues, "the more they change them into apparently inanimate 'things'" (p. 45). On the surface, Freire's sense of possessive consciousness seems to play out solely as an ideological process of objectification: educational processes (forms of learning, teaching, and being) and those involved in education (students, teachers, administrators) are made into objects. Fixed objects, of course, are more easily accounted for and dominated within institutional systems. Yet pushing Freire's concepts a bit further recognizes an ideologically informed sense of desire: in the neoliberal context, not only are people and processes fixed as objects for domination, there emerges a socialized *desire* to fix them. "Fixing" I use here to refer simultaneously to the ideas of *repair* and *making static*. As I noted previously, in the neoliberal context, making static is, in fact, part of the repair. The process takes a technocratic approach to human life (measures of efficiency, procedures of accountability, and the valuation of human capital) and fixes humanity (stasis) while simultaneously fixing (repair) people to fit into the neoliberal order. Through the incorporation of this desire (to fix and to dominate), we begin to see the connection to necrophilia through an ongoing passion to kill (in this sense, to fix subjectivities) and dwell within the dead (accounting for that which has been brought to stasis).

This account of the necrophilic may be just another but more telling way of revealing the end of interpellation: the ideological subjection of the subject. Importantly, ideology calls us into being as autonomous subjects within conservative modernization which we believe ourselves, indeed, to be. For while ideology calls us into being, it does not call to us to say, "Hey, I am being ideological!" In other words, such interpellation is subjection not subjecthood.

To accomplish this, ideology functions together with principles of reification, fetishization, and alienation in neoliberal educational practice. Following the critical tenets of Marxian analyses (alluded to by Freire's earlier notion of possessive consciousness), reification implies a capitalistic transformation of people, relations, and practices into *things* (that, in turn, might be simultaneously quantified, catalogued, and dominated). This *thingification* is a principal mechanism by which humans are alienated from the very processes in which they are immersed. No longer a process in which humans engage, education becomes a series of fixed points external to the learner him/herself. This externalization is made commonsensical through its continued replication throughout educational systems of all levels (primary, secondary, and tertiary). In this way, students are estranged from the "Gattungswesen"—the sense and shaping of self—and see themselves through external technical processes manifesting in technical objects: grading/grades, tracking/label, standardized testing/score.

Also a form of alienation, fetishization situates the individual as a passive consumer of things that are assumed to contain human qualities and values (here, the object is shown to act upon the passive individual, never fulfilling the promises they are made to resemble). Thus, externalized objects, produced by educational systems, are made to represent some future possibility, distanced from their immediate context. As a consequence, as education is reified into a distinct set of consumable objects, so are the outcomes of neoliberal education (degrees, certifications, credentials, and such) assumed to be more than they are; they stand-in for the promise of a better life, a more human existence. This, of course, is exacerbated by privatization of education which, having brought them into existence, now must market its reifications. Again, this is a doubled distancing as educational processes are fixed, externalized, and made to signify more than they are; alienation continues unabated for the oppressed.

While I will have more to say about this in the next chapter, Simon Boxley (2017) points out that because of the standards and accountability movement and the push to various forms of schooled self-regulation, the products of children's and teachers' labor are redefined as a series of performative transactions. However, Boxley is critical of "left-leaning soft-postmodern social critique" that is frequently proffered as "performativity" within the "discourses" that engender performance. So, in relation to the market logic of taking over schools, of course, it is the case that students and teachers begin to perform their roles in particular ways beneath "the gaze" of all the regulatory systems now in place in schools. The point, however, is more descriptive than explanatory because the larger point or context, from a Marxian analysis, is missing: Capitalism. Again, the point of this chapter is to argue that the connection here between the performative and the material conditions of capitalism is best captured in the work of Althusser, especially through the concept of interpellation previously discussed and through the ways ideology functions at the level of the superstructure.

It is the investment and the expectation of returns, the value added, that now drives teachers and students to engage in self-commodification, seeking objective, measurable indicators of their value. As Boxley puts it, "it is not the all-pervasive 'texts' which are 'making this up,' but rather the material practices associated with working under conditions of ubiquitous marketisation" (p. 23). Of course, one of the primary material conditions is the ongoing data-ization or quantification of teachers' and students' work. And, it is here that value as relation becomes quite evident. It is not that one child, drawing on his or her interests or experiences, knows more about X and another knows more about Y and that they are not in competition. It is that both children know more about some predetermined Y and that by some future point this will become $Y + n$ and that one child's n will be greater than another's. As far as the teacher is concerned, the overall average among her students must be that $Y + n$ must not be $Y + (-n)$, regardless of Y.

I say regardless of Y because Y is determined through the material conditions that drive what it means to be educated. In this way, Y must add to the potential of the economy; it must add to the labor capacity of the future laborer. Thus, both Y and students become commodities as human capital theory has long told us. Again, their value as such is measurable and, therefore, increasingly measured as students spend more and more time preparing for, taking, and resting from some or another mis-educative standardized test. As I noted in the example of "value added" provided in Chapter 2 by the Standards and Testing Agency in the UK, this extends all the way down to our youngest laborers. If there is good news here, it is that the increase in testing, the growing emphasis on corporate notions of standards and accountability, and the increasingly intrusive top-down mandates toward these ends are also increasingly visible and notorious. Most teachers (and some parents) recognize these phenomena as problems. It is here, through the visible materiality of ideology, that the possibility for resistance emerges.

While such possibility exists, it is first necessary to recognize the forces at work here. Through the neoliberal mechanisms of contemporary education, principles of reification and fetishization collude to alienate teachers, students, administrators, and community members alike from their own flourishing, from becoming more human. In this way, educational institutions, through the fetishization of dead things as opposed to living education, contribute to systemic inequities even as they are promoted as avenues toward a better life. Yet what is the neoliberal answer to how some "better life" might be achieved? Through taking on the very qualities and identity required for survival in an oppressive system: "In their alienation, the oppressed want at any cost to resemble the oppressor, to imitate him, to follow him" (Freire, 1989, p. 49). Here, identification (wanting to be) with the oppressor forms a third form of alienation, activated and accelerated by neoliberal educational systems. As educational processes and practices are made into desired things, and outcomes determined as desirable abstract ideals, the oppressed seek a way out of their circumstance through obtaining educational commodities that, together, signify their place among the (liberated) oppressor—they thus seek to inhabit the very thing that kills them. Consequently, there exists a circular process of giving life in order to kill (or killing in order to give life) that is necrophilous in origin.

If I have not already intimated sufficiently above, let me argue explicitly that such fetishization is a part of the way that the subject is not subject but is interpellated as such. I draw again on the testing and accountability regime—which now reaches into preschool even as it has precious little to do with benefiting children—to clarify. As Boxley rightly puts it, the "value [of the capacity to labour] has come to be measured by standardized testing arrangements in schools, operating as proxies for employability, and accounting for returns on the state's investment" (p. 137). Schools are, of course, not only academies for labor but sites of labor themselves. And, teachers are called into being, accordingly, as bosses. Consider the strange and terrible symptom of neoliberal fixity that one rarely hears a teacher in a school utter the words, "get back to learning." What you hear from teachers, even good ones, in capitalist schools is "get back to work." Indeed, "carving out and defending the space for the young child to engage in un-alienated free labor—'play' is the more familiar term—is a struggle against the expansive grip of the neoliberal state…" (Boxley, 2017, p. 138).[5] The ability of the child to engage in labor is now referred to as "school readiness," deepening the grip of a totalizing capitalist logic. And even children now relate to each other, at least in schools, in terms of their productive capacity—presented to them as a test score or grade.

This latter form of alienation contributes to horizontal violence which, of course, further ensconces the oppressor. If not a fatalistic consciousness, it is certainly an "adapted" consciousness that prevails. The opaqueness of oppressive social relations is a precondition to serving the interests of the dominant, forcing subordinate groups to seek to move out of their oppressed state through, in turn, oppressing their peers. If they do recognize the double-bind of their oppressive situation, in some state of semi-transitivity, the oppressed still must play the game as written. Here, again and as noted by Willis (1977) previously, we see the competing individualistic and collective goals regarding social mobility wherein some individuals might "make it" while the class system remains tightly in place. Indeed, some individual successes are required for the dominant ideology to gain even tighter hold.

Thus, in order to achieve some semblance of social mobility the oppressed must take on the rule of individuality that stems from a capitalistic culture and, of course, do so at the expense of their own group-based identification. Living one's life or a community living its life through and by the rules over which they have had no say is, logically, cultural invasion. The invaded are interpellated then as conscious choosers, that is, restrained mainly to consumptive choices. Of course, education—as a vehicle of credentialism to pursue the image of the oppressor—is one such consumptive choice. Indeed, as Willis goes on to note, "It is in the school with its basic teaching paradigm that those attitudes needed for individual success are presented as *necessary in general*" (p. 129, original emphasis). As such, traditional schooling must be regarded as an ISA designed to alienate people from their own freedom, enforcing an alienating individuation that maintains the oppressive neoliberal system.

Neoliberalism as Necrophilia and Imperialist Nostalgia

Fromm's use of necrophilia (and biophilia) was made visible during a teaching trip to Paraguay. When trying to find some supplies for class, a student made arrangements to travel to a typical US-style shopping mall. As we approached the mall, he gestured toward it. "This is death," he said. "Go to the old market while you are here. There is life." What he meant, it seems, is that the mall is almost solely about consumption, about fitting into the neoliberal order. The market, on the other hand, is about need, living, cooperation, social interaction, and give and take. It is the making and enacting of culture, not business even as negotiations might be seen as such. That said, the mall itself is also the making and enacting of culture, though seemingly without the historical context upon which the market depends for recognition. But this enactment takes ideological direction, forming the basis of social division. Thus, especially as regards neoliberalism, Fromm, lamenting the dissolution of cooperation and sharing, notes "with the increasing production and division of labor, the formation of a large surplus, and the building of states with hierarchies and elites, large-scale human destructiveness and cruelty came into existence and grew as civilization and the role of power grew" (p. 435). The symbols of necrophilia are today what they were for Fromm, perhaps in intensified form: (1) facades of concrete and steel (especially as they are wastefully destroyed to build new such facades since another symbol is the wasting of resources and consumerism), (2) idolatry of technology, (3) modern weapons systems (especially as they are connected to idolatry of technology, e.g., drones), and (4) treatment of people as things (through either technologism—e.g., murder by drones—or bureaucratism).

We might extend Fromm's notion of necrophilia to point out a simultaneous desire to kill, dwell in death, and mourn what is no longer living. Here, the necrophilous inclinations of neoliberalism draw forth what Rosaldo (1989) termed "imperialist nostalgia" or the tendency to mourn what one kills as part of an imperialistic drive. As Rosaldo writes, "Imperialist nostalgia revolves around a paradox: A person kills somebody, and then mourns the victim. In more attenuated form, someone deliberately alters a form of life, and then regrets that things have not remained as they were prior to that intervention" (pp. 69–70). Given the above example, though the hyper-capitalistic processes of neoliberalism might kill off the "old markets" (now replaced by more efficiently global shopping malls), there remains a nostalgic turn toward what once was before economic values forced independent stores to the periphery. The "old markets" become quaint museums of an economy before neoliberalism, a sideshow to the engine of a now-globalized commerce. Here, the "old market" might be shown as a caricature of what once was, offering a means to nostalgically consider the past even as one engages in the hyper-capitalistic moment of the contemporary now. In short, this is a dual process of creating a new object (the mall) and making it into something more than it is. The mall takes on significant symbolic and ideologically reproductive power as progress in the neoliberal order. Simultaneously, the old is killed or thingified and temporally distanced, feeding nostalgia.

There remains a useful alignment here in regard to neoliberal education as serving the production of a type of *living death*—the object fetishized as more than its material ends, the dynamic process fixed to a point of inanimacy. As Rowe and Klassman (2013) point out, neoliberal educational policies such as No Child Left Behind and Race to the Top emphasize technical skills and knowledges—or, more accurately, different forms of "know-how"—that produce unthinking scientists and educators capable of inventing (and simultaneously abhorring) "havoc-wreaking monsters," non-thinking students whose education emphasizes their placement as "cogs in the engine of global capitalism" (p. 196). Here, students are not animated by any life-giving education but are, instead, reduced to mechanistic movements lacking moral engagement.

Instead of life, students are given "know-how." Know-how forms a line of demarcation between the immense majority of workers who are workers for life and upper-level supervisors. As Althusser (2014) observes, "Some people (engineers, upper-level supervisors and technicians, factory directors and all their assistants) hold a monopoly on certain contents and forms of knowledge, and thus on a form of 'know-how', while others…are penned in other contents and forms of know-how" (p. 38). It is, of course, the role of the school to distribute these forms of knowledge appropriately, the line of demarcation in this process just happens to be both classed and raced (Anyon, 2011). More broadly, however, it is up to schools to "teach" everyone "the rules of good behavior…the properties to be observed by every agent in the division of labour…respect for the social and technical division of labour…and…the rules of the order established by class domination" (Althusser, 2014, p. 51). Such know-how reinscribes the social order, ensuring that education serves the needs of neoliberal processes.

Similarly, Marx (1977) famously wrote, "Capital is a dead labor that, vampire-like, only lives by sucking living labor, and lives the more, the more labor it sucks" (p. 342). The vampire qualities of capital are likewise performed in the educational arena. Indeed, an example of capitalism draining the life of education might be found in van Manen's (1990) recognition of "hopeless hope" as a deteriorating effect of contemporary educational policies:

> The language of objectives, aims, teacher expectations, intended learning outcomes, goals, or ends in view is a language of hope out of which hope itself has been systematically purged. The language of aims and objectives, therefore, is a language of hopeless hope. It is an impatient language that neither bears nor truly awakens. (pp. 122–123)

"Hopeless hope" extends from a capitalistic function that sucks the life out of learning, creating a deadening technocratic system that dwells in an "impatient language" that favors death—the empty production of educational ends that can only be known through an adherence to similarly empty pedagogical and learning practices. From this emptied educational system, then, rises a bureaucratic necessity: the system can only continue through strict accountancy of measures, outcomes, and externalized goals. Certainly, there remains a direct connection from neoliberalism and its guiding corporate-oriented logic of efficiency and accountability to bureaucratism. Bureaucratism is, in turn, supported and exacerbated by technologism—both spaces being occupied by what Michael Apple (2006) refers to as the new managerial middle class. Manifestations of these connections are especially visible in education where, for example, standardized testing (seen by neoliberal policy makers as the most efficient technology of accountability) increasingly drives both curriculum and pedagogy. While not invoking the term, Anyon essentially sums up the context and function of the managerial middle class. Noting the extent to which Race to the Top and No Child Left Behind privatize a number of education functions, she explains, "The laws encourage and support huge increases in private company provision of school services like student transportation and food, test development and preparation, data analysis and management, staff development, remedial services, and content area-specific programming" (p. 75, see also Burch, 2009). In this way, members of the managerial middle class become the human embodiment of the ideology of the superstructure.

Technologies of all kinds may tend toward the automatonization of the subject, thus adapting him/her as object through the very objects that seemingly call him/her into being as subject. Freire sees necrophilia in his description of banking education—to which the testing and accountability movement gives life—since it begins with a false understanding of men and women as objects; static and fixed entities no longer imbued with the potential that is life. This leads to mechanical, routinized teaching which is, of course, exacerbated by such routinized things as standardized testing and competitive grading, pillars of the structures of socialization that underlie correspondence theory.

For the necrophilous character things rule. It is here that Fromm (1973) also helps us to understand neoconservative ideology as necrophilous. For, as he notes, "…the past is experienced as quite real [for the necrophilous character], not the present or the future. What has been, i.e., what is dead, rules his life: institutions, laws, property, traditions, and possessions…the past is sacred…drastic change is a crime against the natural order" (p. 339). As regards education, there is a parallel here in Apple's (2006) description of the neoconservative agenda wherein policy derives from "a past in which real knowledge and morality reigned supreme, in which people knew their place, and where stable communities guided by the natural order protected us from the ravages of society" (p. 39). Of course, it is important to reiterate, to understand the power of the several groups that comprise the conservative restoration, that neoconservatives share with neoliberals the notion that the natural order includes the market economy.

Where Does Althusser Leave Critical Pedagogy?

Understanding the reciprocal relationship between the base and superstructure and blurring the line between them, an Althusserian read of ideology reveals myriad spaces where resistance might occur within the apparati of the superstructure. However, we should be concerned that, while an Althusserian understanding reveals that critical pedagogy cannot deal with the stable, singular notion of ideology present in Marx, it is unlikely to be able to deal with the much more robust notion of Althusser, even as in being more robust, it opens up greater possibility. This is because Althusser's material conditions are in constant motion.[6] The dominant ideology here, unlike in Marx's singularity, functions in myriad ways and responds in a number of absorptive ways. Even as critical pedagogues identify points of intervention—stop tracking, stop competitive grading, stop detention, stop drill and kill and many other performances of ideology—ideological centrifugal force remains to hold the dominant ideology in place. Thus, teachers might resist "drill and kill" and the ease with which that results in the determination of a competitive grade. They might turn to something more progressive such as having students develop, review, and reflect upon a portfolio. But, of course, such practice was easily co-opted such that, for example, portfolios should demonstrate the achievement of "proper dispositions." Through capitalist rationalization, these dispositions are further reduced: We hope you get a "4"; that is "target." But a "3," "developing," is OK too. Patrick Shannon (2007) explains the powers that drive such ideological functioning:

> During the 1980s and 1990s, as the possibilities of composing new curricula and improvising instruction increased, teachers and teacher educators who encouraged them should have expected reactions from the forces of rationalization. And the "empire" did strike back with all its forces. First, textbook publishers absorbed the rhetoric of this resistance into their scripted programs, and the state assimilated the language of resistance into policies without making any accommodations in the expected tested outcomes. Second, philanthropic organizations brokered a consensus that these changes in teaching threatened not only the future of current students, but the economic future of the country as well. Third, business leaders chimed in that they couldn't find skilled workers for the high-wage/high-skill jobs they had open. Fourth with this consensus, government officials called for the reestablishment of standards and accountabilities, and then, funded research to prove the need for both. Finally, many educational psychologists were quick to the funding trough, providing scientific reports discrediting composed curricula and improvised teaching and reaffirming the scientific basis of the commercial scripted programs. Through NCLB

and the Reading First Initiative, the federal government offered underfunded school districts financial incentives to comply. (p. 168)

Thus, we are quickly pulled back into the governing rationality of the policies and practices entailed in the superstructure. As Marx (1978) explains, "The bourgeoisie cannot exist without constantly revolutionizing the instruments of production, and thereby the relations of production, and with them the whole of relations of society" (p. 38). Part of this process, for Althusser, is the constant movement of and revolution of the material practices within ISAs, changes in law, rules, policies, and even the co-option of simple rhetorical devices as exemplified in the new critique among neoliberals of factory schools.

Even as its practitioners recognize the reproductive power of schooling, critical pedagogy seems to entail an underestimation of the dynamic power of education, especially in light of the material reality of schools. In reality, schools remain *re*legitimizing institutionalized spaces: relegitimizing the very structures, policies, and practices (both within and without schools) that critical pedagogy seeks to problematize. In this way, critical pedagogy in schools may be much like teaching a toddler to swim in a bathtub. The toddler will certainly get wet, put her face in the water, and even take a stroke or two. Parents might even explain that this isn't exactly like swimming, ostensibly getting the child to analyze the ways in which the walls of the tub limit and shape the experience. So, along the lines of the soda example previously, even as critical pedagogues might have students analyze, say, standardized testing as a sorting mechanism in service of the neoliberal order, students still take the test and are sorted accordingly, coming, perhaps coercively, to refer to and become data points of hyper-surveillance. Thus, critical pedagogy can become an error of commission to the extent that students simultaneously understand but adapt to the construction of such social relations. Another way to put this is that critical pedagogy "too often privileges the institutional analysis at the expense of existential authenticity, that is the individual person's concern that his or her life is meaningful and fulfilling" (Ross, 2015, p. 215). But even so, to the extent that critical pedagogy reinscribes some illusion of autonomy (the same illusion inscribed by the dominant ideology in the first place in its self-denegation), what is fulfilling may still become an ideological directive. Horkheimer's take on ideology is instructive here. He observes that the structures of production and all of the functions and services and other operations entailed therein are not natural states, emerging—following his Marxian instincts—from the mode of production. In turn, the so-called subject is subjected, as I have argued throughout following Althusser. Horkheimer (1972) put it this way:

> The seeming self-sufficiency enjoyed by work processes whose course is supposedly determined by the very nature of the object corresponds to the seeming freedom of the economic subject in bourgeois society. The latter believe they are acting according to personal determinations, whereas in fact even in their most complicated calculations they but exemplify the working of an incalculable social mechanism. (p. 197)

In other words, students still plop their quarters in the soda machine.

While this is certainly an urgent point, such existential authenticity must derive, in the first instance, from the worth as a human being, not just as a being that produces worth. Here I refer back to my earlier position that class remains the most salient form of structural oppression given the dominant capitalist ideology. While it is also imperative to justice to recognize and deal with other concerns of existential authenticity, this should not distract the left from its Marxist roots and the structural centrality of social class and the pernicious effects of capitalist social relations and how those, now reading through Althusser, manifest and are reproduced in school. Again, while Marx provides an important understanding of the base and why we must engage in critical pedagogy and Althusser expands our understanding of the superstructure and where we can engage in critical pedagogy, the effects, as illustrated through the functioning of imperialist nostalgia and necrophilia, remain limited within the confines of schools. Therefore, in the next chapter, I will argue that we must get students out of school.

Notes

1. It is interesting to note that complaints about factory-like education come from neoliberally oriented thinkers such as DeVos and Duncan (current, as of this writing, and former US Secretary of Education, respectively) and that they are also made by an increasing number of education entrepreneurs.
2. It should also be noted that the "self" described in self-regulated learning is not universal. As Vassallo (2013) notes, "the working class self stands in contrast to the kind of self that underpins self-regulated learning" (p. 572), which is saturated by the values of the white middle and upper middle class self (cf. Lareau, 2003).
3. The point in this example is not to take a side in this particular debate but to, in part, remind of the epistemic humility required for proper development of autonomy and rational deliberation.

4. The discussions of cultural invasion and necrophilia owe to Petrovic and Kuntz (2018) and Kuntz and Petrovic (2018), respectively.
5. The importance of unstructured play to the development of a variety of learning, social, and emotional skills cannot be overemphasized, especially for elementary students. Unfortunately, in the United States, one of the effects of No Child Left Behind has been cuts in recess time (McMurrer, 2007). Further, getting back to the effects of capitalism, it should be noted that children in poverty have less access to such play, fewer minutes of physical activity during the day, and the fewest minutes of recess in school (Ramstetter & Murray, 2017).
6. As an interesting aside, like many pedagogues, Althusser wrote of the productive recognition of posing problems to be solved, an element of "living science" that Althusser distinguishes from the technocratic elements of "know-how" most often taught in schools. For Althusser, this element of problem-posing develops from the material realities of education that seek to materially disrupt the relations of production, not simply reform them (p. 51, n. 6).

· 4 ·

UNSCHOOLING AGAINST THE IDEOLOGICAL STATE APPARATUS

Simplistic renderings of Marxism in critical pedagogy emphasize ideological changes (within education) without linking them to determining changes to the material base, and any claimed alterations to the social system that leaves intact normative relations of production are only reformist in nature and are, thus, easily appropriated into the dominant system of capitalism. Rereading this through Althusser leads to the acknowledgment, however, that the base and superstructure cannot be so discretely separated and that engagement at the level of the superstructure is not merely about reform but also about reinforming an understanding of the base. While reform is insufficient, it is absolutely necessary to a reimagining of the base that motivates the necessity for reform in the first place. In other words, reform, which occurs at the level of the ISA, is unlikely (for Marx) to alter the base and the concomitant social relations. Reform addresses the symptoms and, by not suggesting that something fundamental then be changed, reinscribes existing social relations. But, for Althusser, by engaging the symptoms (e.g., competitive grading), we cannot only realize there is, in fact, something structural that is creating them but also such engagement creates new kinds of voids in the superstructure that might, in fact, reach all the way down. In the end, Marx does not provide a discussion of the superstructure and the ISA that allows us to see the evidence of the base cause of injustice. Arguably, he provides that in other ways (e.g., exploitation) but it isn't particularly informative of how critical pedagogy might engage in schools. Therefore, there is a need to appeal to Althusser and his materialism of the encounter (about which I say more subsequently). Schools manifest as institutional features of society. They are part of the superstructure and, hence, the ideological material. As such, they function as ideological state apparatuses, reinscribing the existing social order. Even with the reconnection of the base and superstructure and the myriad points of engagement such an understanding reveals, in the end, the material conditions within schools (including the apparati of schooling such as the growing testing-industrial complex) may simply overwhelm critical pedagogy which, as a social theory, remains tied to the ideal and abstracted from the material. As Freire (1973) asserted some time ago, "An analysis of highly technological societies usually reveals the domestication of man's critical faculties by a situation in which he is massified and has only the illusion of choice.... He comes to accept mythical explanations of his reality" (p. 34). This is, as I argued in the preceding chapter, how ideology functions.

In this chapter, I want to argue the need to get students out of schools. Here I will draw help from the tradition of deschooling, sometimes referred to more contemporarily as unschooling. This requires, in the first instance, the development of a philosophy of unschooling that accounts for and seeks to rectify the illusion of autonomy brought about through the ideological function of capitalist social relations.[1] To do this, this chapter connects more contemporary work in materialism back to the materialist work of Jean Jacques Rousseau. Specifically, I draw on Freire and Althusser to align materialism with Rousseau's radical roots as an "unschooler." Situating education with the production of moral citizenship, what Rousseau provides that Althusser does not is a philosophy of education that corresponds to the social theory. Rousseau also offers us an element of human flourishing that is not found in either the conservative or criticalist tradition. Linking Rousseau with the unschooling movement blurs the line between formal institutionalization of education and educational practices as they occur beyond the school walls. This philosophy, in turn, maps onto the more contemporary ideal of unschooling, as presented by A. S. Neill (1960), Ivan Illich (1972), and John Holt (2016), among others. In the end, unschooling is a necessary addition, but not alternative, to critical pedagogy to the extent that the latter is consumed within the material reality of schooling and the former represents a mechanism for resisting the necrophilous tendencies of contemporary formations of education in our schools.

Toward this end, I bring seemingly disparate philosophers and social theorists into productive tension, regardless of their historical alignment. Even as, for example, Fromm wrote in the 1970s about capitalism in general and not neoliberalism and even as Rousseau predates the manifestation of neoliberalism, they are speaking about some of the same general issues I have noted to this point. In this sense, though neoliberalism exists as the present context in which we are currently immersed, both Fromm and Rousseau, as well as others, offer a philosophical perspective that productively impacts my sense for how education manifests in contemporary times and, of course, a vision for how it might be different in the future.

A Preliminary Idea of Unschooling

Unschooling is, in many ways, the antithesis to conservative schooling. Two separately developed alternatives to such schooling have contributed to the growth of the unschooling movement: democratic free schools and homeschooling. In free schools and in homeschooling, small numbers of children develop close relationships with caring adults, who are in a position to observe and nurture the interests of each individual child. While the claim may be more generally applicable to free schools than homeschooling since homeschooling and parenting styles vary much more considerably, such approaches are based in social constructivist theories positing that children learn by constructing their own mental models of knowledge and the world, aided by or "apprenticed to" more knowledgeable others. In the development of democratic free schools, children have full control over their time, activities, and decisions; no one tells any child what to do or how to do it.[2] Sometimes children seek suggestions, but they are as likely to consult other children as they are to consult adults at the school. Each child in a democratic free school constructs his or her own mental models; parents learn to respect children and their interests and parents begin to trust children to learn without having their learning managed for them.

An early democratic free school, Summerhill, was founded in England in 1921, and continues today. In the United States, the Sudbury Valley School was founded in 1968, giving children full democratic rights at school, and there are now over 50 Sudbury schools worldwide. Similarly, Italy witnessed the School of Barbiana, based on an ethic of care and freedom, while in Cataluña the brief existence of the "Escuela Moderna" introduced a secular, noncoercive school that relied heavily on excursions and contact with others.

In many ways, life at a democratic free school resembles "unschooling at school" since students attend an actual physical school while decisions about what and how they will learn are left to the children themselves, rather than being managed by adults. Unschooling, then, is a kind of homeschooling that puts motivation and responsibility for life and learning in control of the learner. More than a method, "it is a way of looking at children and at life. It is based on trust that parents and children will find the paths that work best for them—without depending on educational institutions, publishing companies, or experts to tell them what to do" (Stevens, 1994, para. 7).

Of course, a definition such as the one just provided could just as easily describe ideals of progressive education, especially those of Dewey. It could also easily be applied to some versions of homeschooling. In regard to the former, a thorough-going philosophy of unschooling must reject the material trappings of "schools." At some point, however, unschooling as a form of homeschooling, as opposed to a democratic free school to which students actually go, becomes a form of liberal elitism. Most parents are not in a situation to accomplish this. Ultimately, I will suggest that this is inadvisable for other reasons, including those related to democratic education and the development of autonomy. In regard to the latter, this thorough-going philosophy of unschooling will be inconsistent with most notions of homeschooling, at least as homeschooling is traditionally understood. I address this second point next in an effort to provide a more direct definition of unschooling.

Homeschooling Is Unlikely to be Unschooling

While homeschooled students currently represent only 3% of the school population in the United States, homeschooling is growing, albeit slowly—up from 2.2% in 2002 (US Department of Education, 2013). This is true in other countries too, as reports from the UK, for example, indicate as much as an 80% growth rate in homeschooling (Mansell & Edwards, 2016; Teachers to your home, 2018). Causes of such increases are, of course, likely to be somewhat different in the UK. One explanation is that schools in the UK are simply oversubscribed (Yorke, 2017). Nevertheless, other reasons, such as religion, are also cited in the UK as in the United States (Jeffreys, 2015).

Arguably, the homeschooling movement gathered steam in the United States as religious fundamentalist families began homeschooling in order to avoid the curriculum and morality of traditional schools that they considered suspect. In other words, ultra-conservativism is not an infrequent motivator for homeschooling. Today, for example, one popular homeschool site—allinonehomeschool.com—will offer a "curriculum covering science, social studies, language arts, Bible and foreign language (with learning Hebrew). All lessons are based off of the book of Genesis." Or, consider another homeschool curriculum provider—Accelerated Christian Education, Inc.—which claims that "Education apart from Biblical values is not true education." Similar programs exist around the world. The European Academy for Christian Homeschooling, for example, also provides parents a set curriculum.[3]

Whereas democratic free schools do unschooling in school, homeschooling, whether ultra-conservative or not, is largely replicative of traditional/conservative schooling out of school. This is true even for the many homeschooling parents who are secular and drawn to homeschooling as a countercultural experience for themselves and their children. Nevertheless, many homeschoolers, be they ultraconservative or more alternatively and critically oriented, choose to replicate schooling schedules, the division of knowledge into discrete subjects, pedagogical methods, and so forth. In other words, they replicate schooling outside of school, doing school at home with the same material effects. The reasons for this seem to be fairly straightforward. First, there has been a proliferation of web sites that make doing so quite easy, providing complete curricula and guides through the homeschool approval process. Second, following from the thinking of Ivan Illich, it may be that institutionalized notions of "school" and "education" have been reified in a way that has stultified our sociological imaginations around what it means to become and be an educated person. School as we know it—steeped in neoliberal policies, technocratic processes, and spirit-killing practices—has simply become common sense.

Of course, there is a bigger difference in the purpose of fundamentalist and secular homeschooling. The former tends to be a rejection of the development of autonomy and is illegitimate therefore. The latter, while perhaps not a direct rejection of the development of autonomy, arguably undermines autonomy in the same way that schooling does. Thus, it is the case that homeschooling—nonsecular or secular—is not the same as unschooling, even as some such parents may claim to be unschoolers. It is incumbent upon me, then, to lay out a philosophy of unschooling to orient such inclusion or exclusion as well as to signal the potential for rescuing critical pedagogy from the material conditions of traditional schools and their ideological function.

A Philosophy of Unschooling (against the ISA)

Unlike so-called unschoolers who simply do school at home, unschooling parents reject the trappings of traditional school and facilitate their children's interests and activities in ways that traditional schooling cannot. Taken a step further, some families view unschooling not merely as an alternative approach to education, but as an alternative lifestyle in which parenting is not coercive in any domain of life.[4] These families have come to be referred to as "radical unschoolers" (Dodd, 2009). But a coherent philosophy of unschooling, which given the discussion above cannot only *not* apply to homeschooling but also will disallow it, must go beyond the psychological foundation of constructivist learning noted and even beyond the philosophical ideal of providing a democratic education. For while non-coercion and following the interests of children begins a democratic education, a democratic education should also have as its core purpose the promotion of democracy and, even more specifically, critical democracy.

In other words, while freedom generally and the freedom to follow one's interests specifically are necessary aspects of unschooling, it is necessary to the extent that it is corequisite to what should be the overriding concern of unschooling: the development of autonomy. Otherwise, freedom arguably plays to the caprice of children and, to take a Platonist tack, freedom without autonomy is not freedom at all. It is, instead, enslavement to and by one's passions and caprices. This not only affects the so-called free individual but also those around her. Returning to the tenets of Liberalism defined early on, both freedom and autonomy are required for development of the child as a person who is intellectually independent, capable of living and conducting themselves in harmony with others, and can lead a flourishing life while caring for the flourishing of others. So education for critical democracy, an education that promotes autonomy as rational deliberation, is not a purely negative ideal.

Unschooling requires experiences that serve to inculcate specific dispositions necessary to a democratic society. While I cannot pretend to be able to develop a finite list of such things, in addition to freedom, autonomy, and flourishing, I might add equality and the mutual respect of people merely for their personhood, a la a notion of inalienable rights. I might include recognition of diversity of experiences, cultural attachments, religious affiliations, among other things that inform different people's view of a good life. In other words, such differences, then, serve as a foundation for rational deliberation and autonomy. We might include a norm of reciprocity by which "we should not make claims and arguments that cannot be accepted by others unless they already hold fundamental moral commitments about which we expect reasonable people to disagree" (Brighouse, 2006, p. 67). All such dispositions seemed to be entailed in the basic tenets of Liberalism, serving the end of critical democracy in which citizens see themselves as subjects. As subjects, they control their own lives. They understand their society and their role in troubling the assumptions and contradictions inherent to it, especially as those contradictions undermine the autonomy of others. Foremost among such contradictions are the inequalities generated by capitalist social relations. Certainly, then, a democratic education cannot be built on the ideal of freedom alone. Freedom is necessary but insufficient for educating for democracy.

Freedom, Self-Love, and Unschooling

The notion of freedom I have in mind here is exemplified in Rousseau's natural man. Drawing on this notion of freedom, I want, subsequently, to consider more carefully the relationship between freedom and autonomy and the importance of that relationship to critical democracy as well as for critical pedagogy. Since unschooling rejects the formal trappings of schools, this discussion flows logically from the framing within materialism.

In unschooling, the parent/teacher as facilitator combined with freedom of exploration and experience might be considered an extreme form of constructivism, harkening back to Rousseau's *Emile* wherein we "make the acquaintance of the natural man…[for whom] the supreme good is not authority but freedom" (Boyd, 1962, p. 35). Schooling is the opposite of freedom. Initially, the need for unschooling is captured in Rousseau's identification of the need to accentuate freedom in the education of Emile as natural man who lives for himself. But Rousseau (1762a) also asks, "…but how will a man live with others if he is educated for himself alone?" (para. 25). So Emile must live as individual *and* citizen without being corrupted by the society of the latter.

First, the need for unschooling is motivated by the positioning of school as a manipulative rather than a convivial institution. In other words, where Rousseau views society as corruptive of individuals, unschooling advocates such as Illich and Holt point to schools as a—or perhaps *the*—primary source of corruption for many of the reasons that I have raised many times to this point. Therefore, innate human goodness must be developed away from the corruptive influence of society, including schools as traditionally writ. Here we must first, Rousseau (1762a) insists, choose between making a man or making a citizen.

It is in this claim that we see the materialism of Rousseau and some of the intellectual roots of Althusser who considers Rousseau among the first philosophers to conceive the development of society as dialectically linked to its material conditions. Specifically, Rousseau is an impetus for Althusser's aleatory materialism or materialism of the encounter or even Marxism of encounter. Aleatory materialism suggests that there is no natural or rational order (deriving, for example, from divine law) but that the social order is contingent. In other words, the historical trajectory of society can be influenced by human intervention. It is important to note here Althusser's break from orthodox Marxism. As Althusser (2006) notes, "every mode of production comprises elements that are independent of each other, each resulting from its own specific history, in the absence of any organic, teleological relation between these diverse histories" (p. 199). In Marxism, the encounter was somehow predetermined, not aleatory, as Althusser would have it. The contingent nature of history provides possibility for the philosopher who can now think toward its transformation.

Further, Althusser explicitly recognizes an early form of historical materialism (now a Marxism of the encounter) in Rousseau's tracking natural man to civilized man and the imposition of the social contract. Problematically, and related to how Althusser conceptualizes ideology as material, the content of the social contract depends upon existing social relations. As Althusser argues Rousseau's materialism,

> Rousseau conceives history as a process, as the effect, the manifestation of an immanent necessity...[for Rousseau] this process is no longer a continuous linear development, it is a nodal, dialectical process. The clearest feature opposing Rousseau to the philosophers of the Enlightenment is that he does not conceive the development of human history as harmonious. For the philosophers, there is progress of civilization and progress of happiness: for Rousseau this development is antinomic in itself. (Althusser, 2006, p. 111; see also Sotiris' (2014) excellent review of Althusser's reading of Rousseau)[5]

In other words, both propositions are true, even as paradoxical: "The progress of civilization entails the loss of society" (Althusser, p. 111). Further, we might consider that civilization, as a corruption, should not promote one's happiness while being simultaneously necessary to some measure thereof.

For Rousseau, society corrupts by exciting the passions, particularly self-love. From the baby's first tears, we are taught to be selfish and manipulate others to satisfy our desires. But this instinctive "amour de soi" is about the necessity of self-preservation, neither moral nor immoral. Neither is it in consideration of or relative to others. It is only when this amour de soi combines with the power of reason within the collective that it is transformed into "amour-propre," a self-love driven by comparison to others. For Rousseau, in this way, "history has "perfected reason by deteriorating the species" (Althusser, p. 111).

In his first discourse, Rousseau traces this amour-propre to developments in the Arts and Sciences which, not being needs, resulted in pride and vanity. This was because progress here rendered the forest insufficient to assure man's independence, as it was assured for natural man. "Our souls," Rousseau argued, "have been corrupted in proportion to the advancement of our sciences and arts toward perfection" and "luxury, licentiousness, and slavery have in all periods been punishment" for our arrogance (Rousseau, 1964, pp. 39 and 47, respectively). The result of this is a "base and deceptive uniformity" wherein "One no longer dares to appear as he is; and in this perpetual constraint, the men who form this herd called society, placed in the same circumstances, will all do the same things unless stronger motives deter them" (Rousseau, 1964, p. 38). With this, perhaps Rousseau anticipates the contemporary effects of neoliberal ideology, which also requires that stronger motives be put into place—one of the end goals of social justice and critical pedagogy.

In order to put such stronger motives in place, Emile is not subjected to traditional schooling, at least not until such time as a democratic society is achieved. For Rousseau, such a society would enact the general will of the people achieved by individuals acting through reason for the good of the whole. This would be supported by a purely positive education, a la Plato. However, prerequisite to the making of this citizen—such that the democratic society envisioned might obtain—is the making of the person through an education based in freedom, one that should be purely negative to "securing the heart from vice and the mind from error" (Rousseau, 1762a, p. 93). Learning must be restricted only by natural capacities and guided by interest, self-initiated discovery, and practical experience. In true Rousseau-ian form, Illich similarly insists on returning "initiative and accountability for learning to the learner or his most immediate tutor" (Illich, 1972, p. 24). While schooled children are instructed "in their own inferiority," for Emile, "work and play are all the same.... His games are his occupations" (Rousseau, 1762a, pp. 43 and 67, respectively).

Unfreedom and the Construction of Inferiority for Teachers and Students

Contemporarily, we might consider the example of competitive grading as instruction in inferiority and as against freedom, that is, as corruptive.[6] Grading isn't competitive merely because children compare grades and determine who is and who is not "smart," as they do. Grading is competitive because teachers use grading to construct categories of students, categories of A, B, C... students. There is nothing natural, or neutral, or objective about this process. Some might argue that it is objective to state that 9 answers correct out of 10 on, say, a multiple choice test is 90%. You can't be more objective and neutral than that. That, of course, doesn't dull the fact of categorization and the construction of competition. But, more to the present point, consider that 90% is a "B" in many schools. That is certainly and purely arbitrary, not objective. It is very straightforwardly the social construction of "rigor," a corrupt construction necessary to a corrupt society which requires the creation of classes such that exploitation of the lower classes (*a fortiori*, also a social construction) may continue on its merry way. The educational result of such "rigor" in contemporary times is precisely what Rousseau contemned so long ago: "I see everywhere," he said, "immense institutions where young people are brought up at great expense... [where] they will know how to write verses they can barely understand..." (Rousseau, 1964, p. 56). This is a result of banking education reinvigorated by the testing-industrial complex.

In this way, competitive grading simply becomes another technology that helps to drive the standards and accountability movement specifically and, thereby, the neoliberal order more broadly. As much as teachers and students might resist, grades are the new soda. They are a product, a commodity. Much like the long-tailed C of a Coca Cola, grades are forms of advertising, something by which students can sell themselves. And students, even understanding the manipulation they respond to, must play the game. In the previous chapter, I presented a discussion of the "responsibilized" *individual*. Grades are, then, a technology of responsibilization.

In the previous chapter I also noted how self-regulated learning becomes a neoliberal form of responsibilization. With this, students are actually "taught" how to self-regulate. This, of course, takes us away from the natural inclination of children to explore and learn following their interests which entails choices, decision making, and indeed self-regulation without the need for the imposed "rigor" of instruction in such. So, the other side of this coin is that schools undermine in a doubled kind of way their own stated goal. For, as Illich (1972) argued, schooling "pervert[s] that natural inclination to grow and learn into the demand for instruction.... By making [students] abdicate the responsibility for their own growth, school leads many to a kind of spiritual suicide" (p. 27).

Furthermore, the institutionalization of responsibilization also applies to the institution of school itself, which, of course, trickles down to require the pedagogy of responsibilization just discussed. Simon Boxley (2017) describes this in the practice of school self-evaluation (SSE) in the UK. SSE is a brand of value-added drivel which is also connected to teacher pay. In other words, the plan of the New Labour Government (1997–2001) was to link teacher pay to student performance on standardized exams. Thus, students must reach certain thresholds for teachers to receive an incremental pay rise. The criteria of performance are externally imposed and policed through a variety of other mechanisms. Ultimately, Boxley argues, "it is the intention of Government to see an ever closer link between the feedback mechanisms of performance management and the ideational consent assured by these auto-directive mechanisms" (p. 14). In other words, the interpellation of both teachers and students into the logic of capital and competition is not merely an inevitable effect of the material conditions of self-evaluation but a planned outcome. Boxley refers to this as auto-capitalization, noting that "the brutal truth of the regulative mechanisms of school self-evaluation resides in the deep penetration of the logic of capital into the operation of the pedagogical enterprise" (p. 12).

I have also pointed out (Petrovic, 2017) that the technology of SSE is necessarily made possible by several other technologies identified by Ben Baez (2014) including information, statistics, databases, economy, and accountability. As Baez argues at one point,

> In the society of the statistic, it may be that to make any politically significant claim, we must resort to the database. The database allows us to dispense once and for all with the distinction between knowledge and information, for in the

database, and perhaps because of it, knowledge as sets of organized statements that are transmitted systematically is becoming inseparable from its mode of communication, and today it may be impossible to make legitimate knowledge claims without the database…knowledge is being transformed into quantities of information, which then transforms relations between and among myriad institutions and individuals, all of which are being converted into data. So knowledge must now fit new channels and become operational only if translated into quantities of information. (pp. 79–80)

Here we can simply substitute "school" for "society" and "educationally" for "politically" in the first sentence. Children are no longer expected to know but to score. In this way, children, and now teachers as their "worth" is increasingly connected to students' scoring, become a series of data points, feeding a larger database that simultaneously reinscribes a neoliberal need for standards and accountability and imposes a governing rationality: Governmentality by data (cf. Baez, 2014; Kuntz & Petrovic, 2018). It smacks of *A Clockwork Orange* when Boxley frighteningly points out that in the UK "…the Pupil Achievement Tracker now operated by school managements can calibrate with a high degree of accuracy the future success of students using datasets underlain by forty coefficients and modified by confidence intervals and shrinkage factors" (p. 16).

To continue this analogy, teachers become clockmakers, tinkering toward test results, managing their technique over their art, becoming education workers rather than teachers. Of course, their ultimate goal must then be to inculcate children with the same self-regulating tendencies in order to manage their outputs. Further, of course, the logic of the market demands that such management take place in relation to others. After all, competition is key. And there can be no end in sight here. For the logic of the market requires continuous growth. Earlier I noted that education is reified as a consumptive choice and a distinct set of consumable objects. It is important to explicitly observe that grades, standardized test scores, and the quantification of the so-called value added are all consumables, fetishized as knowledge, performance, and human worth. But this "objective" works downward, fetishizing smaller objectives—those necessary to "make the grade"—as learning.

Such fetishization and the fact that young people may "barely understand" does not stall the ever-increasing desire for amour-propre; it kindles it. For it is driven by the search for rigor—arbitrarily identified by a grade as in the example above. But this is further justified through pedagogical lies, a pedagogy of a constructed variance (which, of course, proves rigor). Take the following example: Student, let's call her Anna, comes home with an "F" on a grammar quiz. On this quiz there were a series of sentences in which Anna had to (1) circle the correct verb (learning subject/verb agreement) and (2) underline the subject of the sentence. Now the assignment is set up visually such that anxious or impatient children, knowing what to do from what they see, can jump right in and get started circling verbs: There are two verbs in each sentence divided by a comma and enclosed in parentheses. (You will find such tasks in just about any elementary grammar book.) Given the visual enticement to get started, Anna neglects to underline the subjects. Of course, Anna gets ten points out of twenty: ten correct (verbs) and ten wrong (subjects), hence the "F."

Drawing on at least two pedagogical lies,[7] the teacher, of course, justifies the grade (read: rigorous categorization). The first lie (actually a combination of lies around assessment) is that we have to assess children to know what they have learned. This begs several questions in this case: (1) Why grade instead of assess? These are not synonyms. The answer here traces quite simply back to the necessity to construct "rigor." So the first lie is that we need "tests" (typically identified as such because they entail a grade). (2) Once we understand that test (driven by the need to grade) and assessment should not be read as synonyms, why not complete the assessment? The answer here requires an understanding of what it is that one is assessing. In this case, it was whether or not Anna knew what a subject was and the correct form of the verb that corresponded to that subject. In this case, understanding of both was clearly demonstrated—for how do you get all of the verbs correct without knowing the subject referent? In other words, the student demonstrated understanding on the test but the test was not used to *assess* accordingly. It was used to test, to grade, to categorize—taking us back to the answer to the first question. So, the second lie is that tests are forms of assessment.

By this neoliberal mechanism, children are coerced into locating themselves in the arbitrary academic hierarchy; they have recognized themselves through others (an inevitable effect of schooling as both Rousseau and Illich understood) via the grades that students inevitably compare. These grades are a form of property, the prime mover of inequality—as Rousseau argues in his *Second Discourse*.

It is not at all clear what agentic options any student has in this particular moment of grading. The teacher—getting motivation wrong—might say (in true neoliberal spirit) that students will pull themselves up by their bootstraps and perform better next time. Some students, but certainly not most, do this. But this is in no way agency. It is evidence of corruption. Supporters of the system will dismiss the argument as shrill, but it is evidence of the enforced enslavement of children to the very mindset that sought to test them in the first place. It is the ideological state apparatus at its most efficient. The frequent *a posteriori* justification that following instructions was part of the test simply drives this point home.

Certainly, students often try to make sense of such experiences. Further, even if they don't engage in some form of conscious sense-making (e.g., that's not fair, mean teacher, etc.), there is still meaning in the experience. Perhaps a student just shrugs her shoulders and says that's the way it is. This is clearly not the experience of freedom but of manipulation, manipulation to the extent that, as Illich put it, "School is the advertising agency which makes you believe that you need the society as it is" (Illich, 1972, p. 163). To put this in Freirean terms, school becomes the inculcator of "mythical explanations of [one's] reality," serving to massify or domesticate students' critical faculties (Freire, 1987, p. 34). Part of this process is the teaching of know-how, "but in forms which ensure *subjection to the ruling ideology* or the mastery of its 'practice'" (Althusser, 2014, p. 236). Given the extent of the coercion, manipulation, and "common-sense" inculcating nature of it, this kind of education, then, is the opposite of an autonomy-promoting education. This is so because freedom is corequisite for autonomy to develop.

Unschoolers against the Neoliberal Order

As I have argued at length now, it is the neoliberal order and its radical infiltration into schools that provides the mythical explanations that Freire contemns and the ideological illusions that Althusser asks us to expose. In such neoliberal formations, it is not autonomy that is the concern but autonomy based on a perverse economic rationality that promotes a hyper-individualism wherein individuals "naturally" act in ways that maximize their own personal, economic benefits. As suggested previously, economic benefit can also refer to the "currency" of the school: grades, among other external, manipulative motivations. This rationality is reinscribed given that neoliberalism is effective at "import[ing] economically-determined terms such as 'viable,' 'efficiency,' and 'cost' into previously non-economically-determined spheres (such as education)" (Kuntz, Petrovic, & Ginocchio, 2012, p. 436). Of course, the most cost-efficient way for students to "earn" school currency is to succumb to the rigid accountability schemes that drive schooling.

Even though not explicitly cast as neoliberal, the concern over such forces is evident in the work of unschoolers. Consider, for example, the language in the critique of education by John Holt. He argues,

> Education, with its supporting system of compulsory and competitive schooling, all its carrots and sticks, its grades, diplomas, and credentials, now seems to me perhaps the most authoritarian and dangerous of all the social inventions of mankind. It is the deepest foundation of the modern and worldwide slave state, in which most people feel themselves to be nothing but producers, consumers, spectators, and fans, driven more and more, in all parts of their lives, by greed, envy, and fear. (Holt, 1976, p. 4)

So Holt decries the undermining of autonomy by society or, stated another way, the imposition of a particular kind of autonomy (neoliberal) that is therefore a false autonomy or an autonomy that is a form of constraint. These are the children who "freely" choose, for example, to constrain their interest in schooled, formulaic form to one paragraph consisting of a topic sentence, three supporting sentences, and a concluding sentence. Such "choice," being completely rational within the context, becomes an autonomy of constraint. Or, perhaps this is just a form of neoliberal individuality run amuck, in which people are used as means to ends, thus betraying the more robust ideal of autonomy defined in the first chapter. It is to this, then, that Holt appeals when he argues,

> Next to the right to life itself, the most fundamental of all human rights is the right to control our own minds and thoughts. That means the right to decide for ourselves how we will explore the world around us, think about our own and other persons' experiences, and find and make the meaning of our own lives. (Holt, 1976, p. 4)

The arguments around neoliberalism and autonomy are in large part why Ivan Illich, although he never invokes the terms explicitly either, initially determined to deschool society. Now, societal deschooling is different from unschooling since a version of unschooling can, as in Sudbury Schools, occur *in school*. What Illich originally meant was that school as an institution should be disestablished: "The State," Illich argued, should "make no law with respect to the establishment of education" (Illich, 1972, p. 16).

For "the existence of schools produces the demand for schooling" (Illich, 1972, p. 56). This is an obvious way in which schools become manipulative institutions, much like the automobile industry, as Illich points out, which manipulates peoples' taste toward private cars and against the convivial institution of public transportation. The demand for schooling is a demand for consumption, the consumption of so-called knowledge which is predetermined, prepackaged, and premeasured. Such consumption is necessary for the further consumption of credentials: "compound[ing] the privilege of others with a new title to condescend to the majority" (Illich, 1972, p. 48). Simultaneously, such a consumptive endeavor "serves as a ritual of initiation into a growth-oriented consumer society for rich and poor alike," transforming education along the way from an end to a means. In other words, education is not about humanity, human interest, or flourishing. It is, instead, an economic commodity, and a scarce one at that, required to "make it" in consumer society. On the one hand, I do not want to suggest that the skills necessary to make it economically are not important. Indeed, this is part and parcel of allowing students to pursue their interests in their own ways. Recall that a flourishing life must minimally allow persons to live from the inside out and be comprised of objective goods, goods which include promoting the flourishing of others. On the other hand, to the extent that schools can be seen as institutions of hierarchy, as purveyors of hyper-credentialism, and as focused on the purely pecuniary needs of consumer society and the concomitant development of human capital as opposed to human beings, they not only reflect the extant neoliberal rationality but also reproduce it. A new overriding common sense prevails from within the institution that has proclaimed (and convincingly so) to provide students with myriad ways of knowing. Ideological hegemony at its best.

Overcoming such hegemony was, arguably, a primary motivator of Illich's argument to disestablish schools. In this, Illich points out his notion of disestablishing schools was misinterpreted to mean the elimination of schools.[8] Given that his recommendations for what education should look like never invoke the institution of schools, this would seem a reasonable "misinterpretation." Nevertheless, the point that might be taken here is that societal deschooling should not involve the elimination of unschooling—whether through free democratic schools or radical unschooling. For these ways of democratically deinstitutionalized schooling (the difference between the former and the latter being a matter of degree) promote authentically flourishing lives in which autonomy plays a critical role.

Unschooling, Autonomy, and the General Will

What must occur, then, is critical engagement with the meaning in the experience. This may or may not and need not occur in the exact moment as our experiences are sedimented events that continue to generate meaning. Critical engagement of one's autonomy in such reading of experience seems to be what is missing in Emile's early education in freedom. This is what Freire refers to as conscientization: The process by which people become knowing subjects, becoming aware of their sociocultural and political reality, the contradictions therein, and their capacity to transform that reality. In other words, once in society, how does Emile make sense of his new, unfree condition? How does he engage the manipulative context? This is, of course, the raison d'etre of critical pedagogy.

In Rousseau, we see both educational motive and method. But what is arguably missing, given Illich's more contemporary critique of schooling and the manipulative nature of neoliberalism, is a radical reshaping of autonomy that will speak to the general will in order to avoid that will taking on hegemonic proportion (again, through neoliberalism). It is necessary to recall Counts' critique of progressive education as promoting hyper-individuality from Chapter 1. For Counts, progressive education lacked attention to conviviality, living in the collective. This individual/collectivity problem also motivated Rousseau's project. Grappling with this must lead to the conclusion that even as Emile may now know himself through his freedom, this is not the same as autonomy. His autonomy easily becomes the illusion provided by the neoliberal order, received by him through the illusion of choice which he misrecognizes as freedom. Freire puts it as follows: "In our highly technical world, mass production as an organization of human labor is possibly one of the most potent instruments of man's massification. By requiring a man to behave mechanically, mass production domesticates him" (Freire, 1973, p. 34). In other words, he no longer questions or, as Freire would state it, "problematizes" his social relations of existence. He abides; he has adapted, taking on the now hegemonic rationality. If it is not a system of mass production, traditional schooling with its scripted curriculum, common core, competitive grading, high-stakes testing, organization by grade level, and "egg-crate" factory-esque architecture certainly all too closely resembles mass production. And what of the rationality that comes from such a system? Consider the questions that children ask in school: How many pages does this have to be? How many examples do we have to give? How many points is this worth? It would be peculiar indeed for a student to ask if she can write as many pages as she wants. Her more constrained concerns are perfectly rational within the rationality into which students have been schooled. Notice how efficient such students are.

However, autonomy cannot be relegated purely to the individual self. Again, it must be related to flourishing, including the flourishing of others. For it is only with and among others that one can identify the fair terms of cooperation necessary to developing the capacity for rational deliberation among competing conceptions of the good. The point here is twofold. First, I want to emphasize the need for the education provided to Emile. If schools are sites of neoliberal (or other kinds of) massification, then conscientization would seem to require the pursuit of "the child's first sentiment [which] is self-love." Second, Emile must still face the rationality of the schooling or "education" to which he might have been subjected in the larger society, outside the physical bounds of the school. Here, self-love must be followed by "love of those about him" (Rousseau, 1964, p. 56). In other words, it is a mistake to read Rousseau's individual freedom as autonomy. Individual freedom is necessary but insufficient. Again, the differences among people in society serve as a foundation for rational deliberation and, therefore, autonomy. If we remove Emile from society, where/how does he gain autonomy even as he may gain a strong idea of who he is as an individual, his likes and dislikes, his interests, and his abilities? Emile may know what he wants and to some degree who he is, but he will not know how to deal with society. Autonomy is not an individual attribute; it is called into existence by society. In this vein, Garland, while citing neither, points to both Rousseau and Freire arguing that "The importance of education can be said to be an end in itself prefiguring free social relations of community and reciprocity, comprised of autonomous individuals capable of comprehending both themselves and the world in which they live" (Garland, 2012, p. 30). Some interpretations of Rousseau suggest that the general will is simply what the citizens of the state have decided together. However, within conditions of diversity, Bertram argues that "Rousseau may be committed to something like an a posteriori philosophical anarchism. Such a view holds that it is possible, in principle, for a state to exercise legitimate authority over its citizens, but all actual states—and indeed all states that we are likely to see in the modern era—will fail to meet the conditions for legitimacy" (Bertram, 2012, para. 20).

Notice, however, that these two observations—the conservative nature of mere comprehension combined with lack of state legitimacy—necessarily suggest the need for constant transformation of society through the enactment of one's subjecthood: conscientization. Certainly, part of Rousseau's educational project was, in this vein, to avoid the domestication of man's critical faculties of which Freire and other critical pedagogues warn. Further, Rousseau would see as political failure a state in which it was possible for one portion of the collective to impose its will on the whole (Rousseau, 1762b). The problem here is that any ideological commitment, as I have tried to suggest, disguises itself as will, not imposition. As noted above, amour de soi combines with the power of reason toward amour-propre. Rousseau argues in his Second Discourse that so many "evils are the first effect of property and the inseparable consequence of nascent inequality [born too of property] and it is property that amour propre seeks to protect" (Rousseau, 1964, p. 156). Indeed, such protection became a deliberate project of the rich, "destitute of valid reasons" as to why he should be able to appropriate for himself "anything from common subsistence that exceeded [his] own" (Rousseau, 1964, p. 158). The rich then proclaim to gather everyone under a single supreme power—laws—such that no one can be oppressed.[9] Such nonoppression would, of course, also protect the property of the rich. Thus, Rousseau concludes that "inequality…draws its force and growth from the development of our faculties and the progress of human mind, and finally becomes stable and legitimate by the establishment of property and laws" (Rousseau, 1964, p. 180) – the material manifestations of ideology for Althusser. This process, then, provided the illusion of choice to men "easily seduced" and who "did not have enough experience to foresee its dangers" (Rousseau, 1964, pp. 159–160). Of course, Rousseau continues, "Those most capable of anticipating the abuses were precisely those who counted on profiting from them" (Rousseau, 1964, p. 160).

So where does this leave us in terms of a philosophy of unschooling and how does it help critical pedagogy? Reading Rousseau together with Freire speaks to the need for a more radical pursuit of the general will. Specifically, I am referring back to the collective autonomy necessary to both criticality and flourishing for which education must help students pursue integration over adaptation. The former "results from the capacity to adapt oneself to reality plus the critical capacity to make choices and to transform that reality" (Freire, 1987, p. 4). Unlike the integrated subject, the adapted object can engage, at most, in "a weak form of self-defense" (Freire, 1987, p. 4). An out of school experience, such as homeschooling, that does not promote such integration and the autonomy it entails cannot rightly be called unschooling. Related to this is the fact that unschooling takes a materialist tack in recognizing the neoliberally reproductive power of schools. Given this, in the end, the straightforward implication of a philosophy of unschooling for critical pedagogues is that we must get students out of schools. As Foucault (2003) asserts, "the element that circulates" between individuals and institutions "is the norm…something that can be applied to both a body one wishes to discipline and a population one wishes to regularize" (p. 254). Here, the norm exists as a comparative determination that simultaneously governs individuals and institutions, students and schools. A desire "to regularize" manifests in neoliberal practices of fixity, dwelling in the stasis of statistical placement, for example. Importantly, statistical logic both claims a detached, objective reality (the data say thus and such) *and* stands in as an ethic unto itself: "statistical assertion now takes on axiological dimensions" (Kuntz, 2014, p. xii).

Students are, thus, governed by the "reality" of their educational past, the data points that pockmark their time in school. Importantly, these markings never disappear, only colluding to produce us as students, teachers, productive citizens, etc., subjects subjected to our data-determined past. Returning to Fromm for a moment, there exists a palpable sense that this past is sacred, unchanging, and fixed as a series of comparative points. Further, any future is likewise determined by its relation to this historical data-self: possibility limited by the fixity of the past. As a consequence, radical change is not possible in such circumstances because any significant alteration to what might be would require a simultaneous break with the normalizing past: Fromm's notion of "a crime against the natural order." Such it is that schooling, when understood within the "society of the statistic," becomes a series of normalized necrophilic practices: "the passion to transform that which is alive into something unalive [or fixed]…the exclusive interest in all that is mechanical" (Fromm, 1973, p. 332). Within the neoliberal world order statistical comparison becomes the focal point of this mechanical interest.

Getting students out of schools and bringing them together with myriad others in the community is important both to their freedom and autonomy and the escape from the normalized, data-ized, responsibilized self that such values promote. It also helps to inform the general will in more radical ways toward the collective autonomy identified by Freire, understanding that this also serves the interests of the individual. In Chapter 2, I was critical of some activities suggested by Wink (2011). I should point out that Wink recognizes to some extent the concerns I raised there, especially concerning materialism. As she observes, for example, "The mere momentum of the status quo will keep us in a vacuum unless we walk out the door and seek other ways of knowing" (Wink, p. 114). In a charitable interpretation, we could read Wink as including in the "status quo" the material conditions of schools that reinscribe particular ways of knowing. But this is not so clear. Even as improving the lives of others is a concern, Wink describes Marxist pedagogy as engaging with new ideas, socially generating new knowledge, cogitating, and reading challenging material. Again, from my previous critique, such skills and academic engagements are crucial but insufficient without the walking out the door suggested by unschooling. Thus, on the one hand, students must escape the school to see the broader effects and structural features of capitalist accumulation. On the other hand, while it points to a way to overcome the limiting effects of critical pedagogy in school, unschooling is not the end to the project of reviving critical pedagogy. It is but one necessary means.

The Materialist Problem with Unschooling

The contemporary state is inarguably divided into the factions representative of political failure for Rousseau. This is especially true along class lines—as well as other lines of exploitation and marginalization (through racism, ethnocentrism, sexism, etc.)—an inevitable by-product of the social relations constructed by capitalism. If existing traditional or institutionalized schooling both undermine autonomy and reinscribe current social relations of dominance and if unschooling is to be about the promotion of autonomy, then it can't be properly considered autonomy if the unschooled simply then reinscribe those same social conditions. In other words, a philosophy of unschooling must ask, "autonomy to what end?" Here Illich and others leave us short.

The problem is that the unschooling frame tends to ignore the material conditions and social relations that occur *outside* of schools. Thus, I doubt that current instantiations of unschooling can challenge the contemporary status quo. Therefore, Althusser's dialectical approach to materialism becomes an even more important heuristic for engaging critical pedagogy to productively radicalize the unschooling movement. In other words, it is necessary to understand the corrupting influence of society (a la Rousseau), the way that the dominant social relations function, and the role of institutions, policies, and practices outside of schools that function as ISAs as problematically as the institution of schooling. Beyond schools, Althusser includes among ideological state apparatuses the religious ISA (the system of the different churches), the family, the legal system (laws, e.g., while the courts function as *repressive* state apparatuses), the political system (including the different parties), the trade-union, communications (press, radio and television, etc.), and culture (literature, the arts, sports, etc.)

Given the myriad institutions/apparatuses in *and* out of schools that call subjects into being, it is a mistake to conclude that unschooling is, in fact, radically democratic. Despite the radical concerns expressed by unschoolers, even as they recognize the problematic material conditions *within* schools (and withdraw from them), they underestimate the broader material conditions and sociopolitical milieu within which the freedom (from schooling) that they seek is exercised. In other words, unschoolers have the same problem outside of schools that critical pedagogues have within schools. As Illich (1972) himself recognizes, "the educational institutions I will propose…are meant to serve a society which does not now exist" (p. 105). This, then, anticipates my concern.

If unschooling is to be as radically free as, for example, Illich postulates (Illich never invokes the notion of "school" in the institutional sense in *Deschooling Society*), then education is in the hands of the student and the apprenticer. Illich refers to this model as relying on "learning webs." The learning web is comprised of four networks for Illich: references to educational objects, skill exchanges, peer matching, and reference to educators-at-large. The purpose of these networks is to allow students to pursue their interests, unconstrained. "The creature whom schools need as a client," Illich (1972) argues, "has neither the autonomy nor the motivation to grow on his own" (p. 150).

While still important, there are important problems with Illich's defense of his learning webs. First, Illich seems to confuse autonomy for simple freedom or lack of constraint. With such freedom, the forces of motivation become the same forces that Illich complains about within schools: the neoliberal society that *does* exist. On this account, Illich does not account for the material and ideological realities outside of school, becoming business (or schooling) as usual. Therefore, first, while experiential and relational in important ways that might challenge traditional schooling, Illich's notion lacks principled means and direction to reveal and challenge the socio-spatial contexts that produce schools.

There must be a larger purpose in seeking out myriad "others" in Illich's "learning webs." While necessary, it is not enough for unschoolers to simply pursue their own intellectual interests, in apprenticeship or otherwise. This purpose, the answer to what end, must refer back to flourishing with the concomitant commitment to the flourishing of others. This certainly points back to the education of the citizen as Rousseau set out and points to autonomy. But a thorough-going notion of autonomy requires conscientization.

In short, Illich's attempt to "fix" (repair) schooling does not attend to the multiple neoliberal policies and practices that "fix" (make static) education; Illich does not overcome the necrophilic tendencies of our contemporary moment. Secondly, Illich's emphasis on "self-motivated learning" suffers from the same critique offered for self-regulated learning (of which self-motivation is an integral aspect): it reinforces the principles of hyper-individualization and surveillance that are part and parcel of the neoliberal project. Although we should value the sense of hope Illich provides, such hope requires more direction than Illich offers because of his overreaching zeal to disestablish schools. In line with the spirit of critical pedagogy generally, practices in schools, even as schools are reproductive of the dominant social order, have the potential to challenge that order. Against critical pedagogues, and drawing on Illich and others, that challenge cannot manifest completely within and through schools, even those wherein critical pedagogy is practiced.

Notes

1. The original iteration of such a philosophy owes to Petrovic and Rolstad (2017).
2. Of course, this is not complete freedom and follows a principle of negative freedom.
3. This is not to suggest that all homeschooling labeled as Christian is necessarily ultraconservative.
4. Here unschoolers beg the question of whether or not coercion is always negative. I should, obviously, coerce my child, even with physical force, not to touch a hot stove even if her touching the stove would lead to learning.
5. *Rousseau conçoit l'historie comme un processus, comme l'effet, la manifestation d'une nécessité immanente. Et en cela il reste dans le contexte de l'Aufklarung. Mais ce processus n'est plus pour Rousseau comme pour les Lumières un développement linéaire continu, c'est un processus nodal, dialectique. Le trait le plus net qui oppose Rousseau aux philosophes des Lumières est qu'il ne conçoit pas le développement de l'histoire humaine comme harmonieux. Pour les philosophes, il y progrès de la civilisation et progrès du bonheur: pour Rousseau ce développement est antinomique en lui-même.*
6. See, for example, Kohn's (1999) discussion.
7. For further reading of interest here, see Krumboltz and Yeh (1996).
8. See the foreword by Illich in Hern (1996).
9. This was, of course, a flawed social contract for Rousseau (1762b), leading him to write his alternative conception in which he famously observes that "Man is born free, and everywhere he is in chains."

· 5 ·

UNSCHOOLING IN AND OUT OF SCHOOLS

> Humanitarian feelings cannot be developed from books, if all the life outside school acts in an opposite direction. To be real and to become active qualities, the humanitarian feelings must arise from the daily practice of the child.—(Petr Kropotkin, cited in Stenglein & Mader, 2016)

As I have argued from the beginning of this volume, a process of normalization manifests in the material conditions in which students find themselves immersed (schools and the policies and practices—the ideological fabric—that make the institution). But, these same conditions also provide the very basis for a resistive sense of schooling not inevitably governed by the society of the statistic. In order for critical pedagogy to have an effect, it, on the one hand, cannot surrender the material space of the school (as some unschoolers and/or homeschoolers would have it) or relegate it to the back-burner of social analysis (as many critical pedagogues seem to do through a shallow rationalism). Nevertheless, Hegel's dialectic—ideal or material—is still important, ideals are still important, questioning, reflection, and action are still important. Furthermore, resistance, even though always at the precipice of co-option, is still important. And these all can take place and be inculcated in the operational space of organized schooling.

In other words, despite the concerns I have raised about critical pedagogy, there is hope and possibility in the space of schools. To demonstrate this, I turn to an analysis of education that pulls from the principal tenets of critical geography.[1] This extends the materially grounded analysis from Marx and Althusser to unfix the fixed education that serves the neoliberal project in favor of a materially based possibility of a new educational dialectic between schooling and unschooling. Edward Soja (2010) posits the socio-spatial dialectic, which I think is entailed in this new educational dialectic, as pivotal to activating progressive social change. The critical geographical perspective affords a materialist perspective that, in turn, presents possibilities for being other than we are (both socially and materially).

Critical geography begins with the premise that social justice work requires a respatialization of our world, one that is not developed by the normative logic and values of our times. But, it is also necessary to recognize that such work is always contingent and a product of the encounter. Thus, bringing Soja and Althusser together highlights the aleatory nature of critical geography that understands the socio-spatial not only as multitudinous but also as in constant encounter.

In *Seeking Spatial Justice*, Soja (2010) links materialist elements of spatial analysis with possibilities for social justice: Through a materialist engagement with issues of inequity, previously unrecognizable possibilities for resistance are made manifest. As Soja points out, other contemporary scholars have similarly addressed normative neoliberal values and assumptions through linking the spatial with opportunities for justice.

In an editorial for a special issue on space and justice in *Critical Planning* the editors point to a necessary overlap in considerations of space with opportunities for justice: "space—like justice—is never simply handed out or given...both are socially produced, experienced, and contested on constantly shifting social, political, economic, and geographical terrains...[consequently] justice...must be engaged on spatial as well as social terms" (cited in Soja, 2010, p. 28). The editors go on to note that just spaces are "necessarily kept open, but must be rooted in the active negotiation of multiple publics, in search of productive ways to build solidarities across difference" (p. 28). Neoliberal values promote closed spaces—spaces that contain, control, and discipline the actors emplaced within their boundaries. Certainly, education offers a powerful example of such circumstance. Therefore, a materialist examination of schooling that points to the possibilities for open spaces is required. In the end, in order to be productive such spaces must be actively negotiated and made radically public.

In order to enact his materialist analysis, Soja (2010) engages a *socio-spatial dialectic* as a means to recognize "a mutually influential and formative relation between the social and the spatial dimensions of human life, each shaping the other in similar ways" (p. 4). In this instance, Soja points to a relational materiality, a firmly entangled production of meaning-making that is simultaneously both social and spatial in origin. Through interrogating the relation inherent within the socio-spatial dialectic, Soja points the way toward productive social change, a means to "increase the possibility of opening up new ways of thinking about the subject as well as enriching existing ideas and practices" (p. 13).

In many ways, Soja's work extends previous scholarship of notable theorists such as Henri Lefebvre and David Harvey, who likewise begin with the presumption that "we make our geographies just as it has been said that we make our histories, not under conditions of our own choosing but in the material and imagined worlds we collectively have already created—or that have been created for us" (p. 18). Importantly, like Lefebvre and Harvey before him, Soja (2010) moves away from a deterministic relation of space, claiming that unjust "geographies and their effects can be changed through forms of social and political action" (p. 20).

As Althusser, there is contingency here, the encounter is aleatory, not deterministic and can be influenced by human intervention. Soja's social and political action creates what Althusser refers to as a "swerve." Building on Epicurus' theory of the formation of the world, Althusser argues that there occurs,

> an infinitesimal swerve [déviation]; "no-one knows where, or when, or how" it takes place, or what causes an atom to "swerve" from its vertical fall in the void, and, breaking the parallelism in an almost negligible way at one point [sur un point], induce an encounter [rencontre] with the atom next to it, and, from encounter to encounter, a pile-up [carambolage] and the birth of a world—that is, of the aggregation of atoms induced, in a chain reaction, by the initial swerve and encounter. [Thus] ... the origin of every world, and therefore of all reality and all meaning, is due to a swerve....
> (cited in Suchting, 2004, p. 10)

The swerve produces an encounter. Taking political action creates an encounter that would not have otherwise occurred. It is such encounters that endow "the atoms" with reality. Even as every encounter is also aleatory in its effects, changing our geographies is a necessary attempt to generate the swerve, creating a new void into which the atoms might fall. In other words, the geographies of schooling (and their effects), though seemingly static, can be changed, a radical possibility for being otherwise might well emerge as a project for social justice work. This is precisely why it has been so necessary to map and name the many static spaces of schooling and why I will continue to do so in this chapter. The materialist work of mapping both attends to the (nearly overwhelming) manifestations of neoliberalism within education and identifies inconsistencies and contradictions within the neoliberal project wherein progressive change may occur.

As Soja (2010) notes, some critics who foreground spatial engagements as a means toward social justice articulate a "vigilant defense of public space against the forces of commodification, privatization, and state interference" (p. 45). Similar arguments might be found in critical engagements with schooling as activists (rightly) question the erosion of the public space of the school (e.g., shifts of public funds to charter schools or vouchers for private schools), its commodification and privatization (e.g., the influx of companies such as Pearson in the testing industry or the rise of for-profit EMOs discussed in Chapter 3), and state interference in course texts (the means by which the state asserts select content as valid [such as intelligent design] and others as questionable [such as evolution]).

Soja (2010) holds a belief in the promise of the materiality of cities to instigate productive social change; schools might be shown to occupy a similar place. To paraphrase Soja, things do not just happen in schools, they happen to a significant extent because of schools. Herein lies the productive possibility of schools to activate progressive social change through their very material presence.

As importantly, Soja (2010) returns to the public's "right to the city" as a basic assumption that fuels his social justice initiatives. This, too, can be applied to schools: the democratic public begins with a basic "right to the school" which, in turn, must extend back into the city. Like Soja, this assertion carries with it a materialist recognition that "the school" is multiple, including material elements of space and the social imaginary of what schools can be and should do. The "right to the city" is an ongoing challenge to the contemporary bureaucratic society that manifests through the state and market infusion into everyday life (Lefebvre, 1991). But, more than just a challenge to the status quo, the right to the city carries with it promise. More than just containing public spaces that must be defended, the city itself manifests as deeply public.

Iris Marion Young (2011), for example, posits city life "as a vision of social relations affirming group difference" (p. 227). Here Young offers a different conceptualization of community away from a totalizing groupness toward a differentiated togetherness. This togetherness of strangers "situates one's own identity and activity in relation to a horizon of a vast variety of other activity, and the awareness of that this unknown, unfamiliar activity affects the conditions of one's own" (p. 238). A right to the school, then, means bringing this variety and the unknown into the school. In doing so, the "right to the school" becomes a challenge to the necrophilic tendencies of neoliberal education: a movement against stasis.

The Aleatory Geography of Unschooling as Critical Pedagogy

In order for critical pedagogy to take hold, it must break free of the centrifugal force of normalization, especially as this dizzying and numbing repetition occurs in and through schools and schooling. The socio-spatial dialectic necessary to this project can be activated by making the school radically public: bringing the public to school and the school to public. Here Soja's (2010) belief in the promise of the materiality of cities to instigate productive social change is important as schools might be shown to occupy a similar place. As Kuntz and Petrovic (2018) point out,

> Soja (2010) repeatedly returns to the public's "right to the city" as a basic assumption that fuels his social justice initiatives. Here, we make a parallel assertion: the democratic public begins with a basic "right to the school" which, in turn, must extend back into the city. Like Soja, our assertion carries with it a materialist recognition that "the school" is multiple, including material elements of space and the social imaginary of what schools can and should be (and do). (p. 71)

Arguably, Eric Sheffield (2011) begins the operationalization of this ideal with his notion of "strong community service learning (CSL)." Strong CSL can bring the outside world into the school and vice versa. Until schools are made radically public in this or some other way, critical pedagogy may become an error of commission, to the extent that, as I have argued previously, it provides only the illusion of autonomy. As I opened this volume, Shaull's point about the non-neutrality of the educational process is worth citing again at this point:

> Education either functions as an instrument which is used to facilitate integration of the younger generation into the logic of the present system and bring about conformity or it becomes the practice of freedom, the means by which men and women deal critically and creatively with reality and discover how to participate in the transformation of their world. (in Freire, 1989, p. 15)

On the one hand, as critical pedagogues, we must recognize the need for the institution of organized schooling since it is there that pedagogy can be given direction to deal with reality. Schools can be sites of critical reflection. They provide an organized place wherein the contradictions of dominant social relations can be revealed and the practice of critical analysis engaged. On the other hand, unschoolers recognize the power of the material conditions within schools. It is, therefore, unschooling that educates or creates the persons as free subjects. Drawing on Althusser, I asked in the introduction: "What is the role of unschooling vs. schooling in the interpellation of the subject?" A response to this question possibly leads to a foundational swerve capable of opening up important voids on both sides of the question.

In answer to this question, I noted in the previous chapter the ways that both Rousseau and Freire spoke to the individual-collectivity problem: Both sought the formation of autonomous subjects as well as engagement with the collective. Arguably, Rousseau was more radical in method vis-à-vis the individual and his freedom and, thereby, more closely aligned with a notion of unschooling. For Rousseau the experience of freedom helps call the individual subject into being as free, knowing the self. Freire was more radical in purpose vis-à-vis society and a vision of autonomy. For Freire, a more formal approach to education, through critical pedagogy, engages and nurtures one's critical capacity in relation to others and to the sociocultural and political spaces one occupies. As such, the now subject seeks to effect just change in those relations and spaces. Such praxis is made stronger by experiencing new spaces in which different social relations manifest. Thusly, new theorizations arise to challenge domination (Horton, Kohl, & Kohl, 1990).

With this, I suggested that a philosophy of unschooling in this vein will render some forms of homeschooling illegitimate, just as it does most forms of schooling. In other words, such a philosophy clearly has implications for the legitimacy of traditional, formal schooling. Certainly, formal schooling is a potential site of resistance in which the focus should remain on developing the person to see herself "to be a maker of the world of culture, by discovering that [s]he...has a creative and recreative impulse" (Freire, 1973, p. 47). This is "natural man," who comes to flourish through his autonomy driven by his freedom, experience, and integration.

To the extent that it does not and cannot provide this, the elaborate, institutionalized apparatus of elementary and secondary schools, reputedly in place to prepare children for college access, may already be counterproductive to the project of facilitating children's development as subjects. While there may be some latitude, especially at the classroom level, such institutions that are inherently conservative—bureaucracy, rules, management, schedules, accountability schemes, etc.—necessarily abound. Even the physical spaces engender certain "managed" behaviors and demand particular kinds of rules (cf. Kuntz, Petrovic, & Ginocchio, 2012). The spaces, rules, procedures, resources (or lack thereof), and numbers of students all collude to call teachers and students into being in reductive ways. Try as they might with the little latitude they have, the educators who occupy such spaces are not Rousseau's tutors.

This is a primary reason that a thoroughgoing notion of unschooling which "puts the desire, drive, motive and responsibility for life—this thing we call learning, or education—in the hands of the learner" begins without schools.[2] That is to say that, much like Ivan Illich's pursuit of "deschooling," it is conceivable that education might occur without institutionalized schools, the existence of which, as noted previously, creates the demand for schooling and all the prepackaged knowledge and credentials (as commodities) that come with it. The alternative for Illich was to disestablish schools—by which he meant that the state should make no law with respect to the establishment of education—and to pursue webs of learning, in which children would interact with adults in real-world situations, learning prerequisite skills for and learning about different jobs, crafts, or professions. In this sense, Illich might be shown to seek the removal of public education as an ideological state apparatus.

Given the choice to remove education from the specter of institutionalization, it is hard to see how such a notion of unschooling does not devolve ultimately into mere apprenticeship, begging the questions of where, how, and when students are educated for democracy as engaged citizens. This may be why Illich (in Hern, 1996) later asserted that doing away with schools is not what he meant by disestablishment and that schools might still exist. Of course, to my mind, they certainly should. For the dominant ideological commitments take even greater hold in such an educational project as the thorough-going notion of unschooling that Illich was initially read to have endorsed. One need only look to the homeschooling movement to recognize the ease with which families "opt out" of public schooling in order to ensure their children take on the conservative ideologies they espouse. As noted in Chapter 4, a great number of homeschoolers assert their conservative religious values as a rationale for removing their children from the public system. Furthermore, even those parents who might opt out for more progressive reasons encounter the material conditions of neoliberal ideology outside of school. It is this consideration that Illich and unschoolers generally ignore. Given this, institutional schooling must have a place with unschooling if schooling is to be unfixed.

This said, traditional schools must move toward being much more like democratic free schools in which children have full, or at least much greater, control over their time, activities, and decisions. This kind of freedom is necessary to the development of autonomy and, therefore, begins to set the conditions within which critical pedagogy can take hold. What I am advocating for, in different words, is the promise of *unschooling in school*—a radicalization of the public spaces of education that makes possible the very critical democratic tenets that Illich seeks in his early vision of destroying educational apparati in the name of unschooling. The point for unschoolers is that children follow their interests. Furthermore, choices that do not involve an apprenticer per se would still follow an adult guide (a parent or other authority figure). Thus, there is not complete freedom but a general principle of negative freedom such that the student comes to no serious harm and avoids harming or interfering with others.

Even so, moving further from the more thoroughgoing ideal of unschooling toward unschooling in school is necessary not only for the reasons already suggested but for concerns about when and how children would learn basic skills, where and how they would engage with and against dominant ideological commitments toward the fostering of autonomy (freedom of choice being not a synonym but a necessary condition), and the need for a somewhat more structured environment in which to achieve these necessary pursuits. Of course, there is a tension here in that such structure may beg my own critique. It is nevertheless and paradoxically the case that some such structure may be necessary to reveal (oppressive) structures themselves, to expose students to them, and to see through their opaqueness. Though perhaps overly idealistic, the possibility remains for radically democratic spaces for schooling to resist fixing identities and processes as a matter of course—unschooling in school perhaps paves the way for education as democratic action.

This, then, suggests a somewhat different model from unschooling in which each child constructs his or her own mental models and parents and other guides learn to respect children and their interests trusting children to learn without having their learning managed for them. In this way, unschooling in school is certainly not a new idea but a derivation of the democratic free school model reviewed previously. Building on this, it is important to note that while negative freedom is important, it cannot be purely so as to leave the development of autonomy contingent to the apprenticer or, worse, to the dictate of the dominant ideology which uncritically calls students into being as subjects for the purpose of subjection. This, I argued, is one way that ideology functions. Here, then, the need arises for some form of organized educational space designed to foster freedom and autonomy which are required for development of the child as a person who is intellectually independent, capable of living and conducting him or herself in harmony with others, and can lead a flourishing life while caring for the flourishing of others. So education for critical democracy, an education that promotes autonomy as rational deliberation, is not a purely negative ideal, requiring, therefore, a certain amount of structure or, dare I say, institutionalization.

A method of unschooling in school that overcomes or at least attempts to reveal the manifestations of the extant material conditions within schools as institutions will require experiences that serve to inculcate specific dispositions necessary to democratic society outlined in the previous chapter. This requires integration, the making of subjects who control their own lives, within and through an understanding of the larger material realities that limit them. They come to understand their society and their role in troubling the assumptions and contradictions inherent to it, especially as those contradictions undermine the autonomy of others, and find their humanity.

This sketch of *unschooling in school* suggests a necessary engagement with both freedom and the development of autonomy simultaneously. While still engaging traditional critical pedagogy, this approach, unlike traditional critical pedagogy, invokes the school as an entry point for social change that works to radicalize the very system of which it is a part. But again, given the material conditions of schools, this approach remains insufficient, requiring some form of unschooling or deschooling. In short, we must get students *out* of schools part of the time. However, as I have observed, even as unschooling may be a departure from traditional schooling, it simply does not account for the material and ideological realities *outside* of school, becoming business (or schooling) as usual. Therefore, the unfixed school requires both unschooling in *and* out of schools. Thus, in the next two sections of this chapter, I will try to operationalize unschooling in school and, then, unschooling (out of school) in an attempt to reveal the promise of this dialectical tension. For the latter, I turn to the vehicle of service learning to bring unschooling into the fold in terms of what counts as "in school."

Operationalizing Unschooling in School

Unschooling in school must be part and parcel of the project of critical pedagogy. Unfortunately, it is necessary to state for conservative readers that this also includes commonsensical undertakings such as basic numeracy and literacy. More than tongue-in-cheek, this is a serious, perhaps intentional, misreading of critical pedagogy by conservatives, to which critical pedagogues must be prepared to respond. To wit, George Will (2006) complained that "the University of Alabama's College of Education proclaims itself 'committed to preparing individuals to'—what? Read, write and reason? No, 'to promote social justice, to be change agents, and to recognize individual and institutionalized racism, sexism, homophobia, and classism,' and to 'break silences' about those things and 'develop anti-racist, anti-homophobic, anti-sexist community [sic] and alliances'" (para. 3). Such conservative nonsense revealed and now aside, let me turn to the purpose at hand: unfixing schools. Some of the structures of fixity within schools, such as grading and tracking, I have raised many times. Unfortunately, the list gets longer. Let me begin by rehearsing the need for critical pedagogy.

Engaging Critical Pedagogy

As I spent significant time to provide the theoretical underpinnings and purposes of critical pedagogy in Chapter 2, I simply build on that discussion briefly here. The skill of and capacity for reflection is a key component. Reflection should invoke dialogue among students and stakeholders alike, lead students to see a problem or contradiction in their experience, make them imagine a solution, get them to apply their academic learning to possible solutions, lead them to test their plan in the problem situation, and get them to reevaluate the problem toward individual, communal, and structural transformation (Sheffield, 2011). The development of this capacity must be a prime concern for teachers in schools, and this development is enhanced out of schools—a point I return to in the next section.

While action toward structural transformation cannot take place in each and every lesson, the point of a good education should be one of building toward this. In this vein, I am reminded of Bank's (1994) four approaches to multicultural education: contributions, additive, transformation, and social action. The first approach is what has been referred to as the heroes and holidays approach (cf. Lee, Menkart, and Okazawa-Rey, 2011) that invokes discrete cultural elements, effectively essentializing and fetishizing diversity. The additive approach is when content, concepts, themes, and perspectives are added to the curriculum without changing its structure. In the transformation approach, the structure of the curriculum is changed to enable students to view concepts, issues, events, and themes from the perspective of diverse ethnic and cultural groups. Finally, in the social action approach, students make decisions on important social issues and take actions to help solve them. Critical pedagogy begins, or should begin, at the transformation approach. Again, this should be seen as over a period of time; not every lesson, project, or class day requires viewing themes from different perspectives. Some days spending time memorizing one's multiplication tables is sufficient and, of course, important. But the point is that the teacher who does not hold the trajectory of their course toward reflection and transformation is not a critical pedagogue. And the teacher whose class never takes action is not a critical pedagogue.

Importantly, for critical pedagogy to push toward a notion of unschooling in school, it must address the structures of fixity that exist within schools. This must be actively redressed by challenging a great number of internal structures including, but by no means limited to, tracking, prescribed curricula, the artificial distinction between work and play, a lack of community involvement, and emphases on tests and grading, among other structures of fixity. As I have spent some time in previous chapters condemning the violence of testing and grading, I will briefly address the first three issues in turn, before moving to a more thorough treatment of community involvement.

Detracking

In Chapter 3, I noted that one of the ways that ideology functions is through dissimulation—by which relations of domination are hidden or obscured or even denied. The example provided was tracking. I also noted the reproductive function of schooling. In this process, tracking not only becomes a structural arrangement that contributes to that function but also relates now to the ideological function of legitimation. In a pernicious cycle, tracking as policy legitimizes students' academic location while legitimation reinforces the policy—now one's social role and socioeconomic status, usually the same as when one entered school, is accepted as inevitable. After all, students were told who they were and would be in school. But it is important to recognize that legitimation does not only affect historically marginalized and underachieving groups. Indeed, what is reproduced in schools in this vein is an "understanding" by students from dominant cultural and socioeconomic groups about who "those" students are. In tracked schools, students begin to focus their interest only in the performance of their own tracked group. This is especially true of students in higher tracks and has a negative effect on low achievers (Meijnen & Guldemond, 2002). As it tends not to occur in more homogeneous settings, this effect should give those of us educating for democracy great pause and provides further evidence of the negatively reproductive effects of tracking. Given this, detracking must be a part of any attempt to unschool in school.

As Rubin (2006) offers, detracking efforts range from deep restructuring efforts (i.e., no tracking) to maintaining tracks while promoting more access to higher tracks for underrepresented students. It seems to me that the latter, while perhaps an improvement, does not fundamentally change the material, policy, and pedagogical conditions. As such, such efforts are inevitably reproductive of the dominant ideology. While the research is still mixed, a growing amount of evidence suggests positive effects of heterogeneous grouping on academic achievement for lower-achieving students (Fauziah & Latief, 2015; Murphy et al., 2017; Venkatakrishnan & William, 2003). The research on high-achieving students is also mixed, with research finding a negative effect on high achievers in *homogeneous* groups (cf. Boaler, Wiliam, & Brown, 2000) as well as a small negative effect from *heterogeneous* grouping (Argys, Rees, & Brewer, 1996). Overall, the best that might be said is that homogeneous grouping has a slight but usually statistically insignificant positive effect on high achievers and a more demonstrable negative effect on low achievers. Given this, critical educators must consider the trade-off that is being made in other terms, especially as regards high achievers. Is it worth interacting with and understanding people from different backgrounds? This, of course, is related not only to intellectual difference but difference more generally as tracking is known to be linked to in-school stratification along racial, ethnic, and socioeconomic lines (Burris, Welner, & Bezoza, 2009; Oakes, 2005). Thus, Hattie (2009) concludes that tracking has "minimal effects on learning outcomes and profound negative equity effects" (p. 90). Thus, to return to the questions about such a trade-off: Is it worth learning to care about others different from oneself? Is it worth seeing how the flourishing of others impacts one's own? Is it worth inculcating—in a real, lived way—the habits of mind and interaction necessary to robust democracy? If we cannot answer with an unabashed yes in each instance, then democracy is already in peril.

All of this said, detracking is fruitless without pedagogical change, as critical pedagogy tells us. Freedman, Delp, and Crawford (2005) noted that effective teaching in detracked classrooms is based on seven key principles: (1) building a long-term curriculum, which promotes the recycling of structures and ideas, with room for ever-deepening levels of complexity, (2) considering learners to be in control of their learning and building structures that support them in challenging themselves, (3) building a learning community that respects and makes productive use of diverse contributions from varied learners, (4) providing opportunities for diverse ways of learning, (5) providing support to individuals as needed, (6) challenging all students, and (7) keeping learners actively involved (pp. 118–119). These are all, it seems to me, elements of what has typically been seen as "good teaching" generally. However, without critical pedagogy, "good teaching" may be simply reproductive within the historical materiality of the school. Detracking adds the dimension of the deep restructuring necessary to changing that materiality and challenging the status quo.

Unfixing the Curriculum

One of the reasons that tracking is able to take hold is due, in part, to the idea that the curriculum must be fixed. Beyond ensuring basic numeracy and literacy, there is no need for curricula to be so thoroughly prescribed as it typically is. E. D. Hirsch provides a quintessential example of such prescriptivism in his notion of cultural literacy. Interestingly, Hirsch's curriculum is not merely overly prescriptive, but archaically descriptive—descriptive of the curriculum of his youth, and, for that matter, of generations before. Even as he says it could be something different, he offers no such alternatives and clearly has something specific in mind. In fact, an alternative that would satisfy Hirsch's primary psychosocial justification for cultural literacy would be to have students watch certain television programs in common (see Howe, 1997; Petrovic, 2001, 2003 for similar critiques). Such formal curricula, often driven by the textbook industry and its whitewashing of all things interesting, quash the interests of children, that which animates them in first place. Therefore, there should be no prescribed curriculum, at least in elementary school up to a certain age range.

Apropos to this, schooling has become fixated, in typical technocratic fashion, on something called "grade level." It is simply not the case that all children should be required to read or do math or anything else at "grade level" by "grade three" (whatever such referents mean). In other words, there can be no truth to a book titled, for example, "*What Every* [insert ordinal number here] *Grader Should Know.*" While merely providing additional exposure to reading materials may not be enough to support early literacy development (Neuman, 2017), we know, for example, from book flood approaches, that children's interest in reading increases with opportunities to engage with interesting reading material and this occurs with little direct instruction (Baker, Dreher, & Guthrie, 2000; Neuman, 1999), including for second language learners (Elley, 2000; Mangubhai, 2001). We should, in fact, "flood" classrooms with all kinds of materials. Children should have primary, although not exclusive, voice in what ideas, activities, and subject matter with which they wish to play.

In play, children are in association in ways authentic to their being, as opposed to the artificial space of school/learning. They must, therefore, begin already to take each other's interests, needs, and flourishing into account, even if, early on, only in terms of the need for negative freedom. As students mature, they might be exposed to different kinds of academic floods, such as projects in sociology (e.g., around issues of race or gender) or projects in economics and politics (e.g., around issues of poverty, election fraud, the imposition of political spectacle over debate since the rise of the Presidential Debate Commission). They might, in this development as subjects, choose to take action. As Anyon observes and as was demonstrated with the Mexican-American studies program in Tucson, "studies have documented that such civic activism…typically fosters [students'] positive personal development, and improves their academic engagement and, therefore, achievement" (Anyon, 2011, p. 102).[3] The ways that students engage, the battles they choose and why, the political (and other) commitments they make are the enactment of autonomy.

Playing Learning

One of the problems here is that schools create an artificial distinction between work and play, a distinction that gains normative traction in the spatial separation of such activities. Work happens in the classroom and play on the playground. Children are frequently chided to "do their work" or "get back to work." It is important to note that this typically involves restricting children's freedom of movement and communication. Strangely enough, the docile student is read as the engaged student.

Learning, like play, is naturally animated, until situated in the unnaturally static space of school where it becomes work. Here, the socio-spatial relation of school fixes learning, rendering it lifeless. Play occurs outside of school bounds (or, though increasingly infrequent, outside during recess) or, if brought into the confines of the classroom, play becomes regulated (think here of the movement to regularize productive forms of play as elements of a prescribed school curriculum).

While play, as we typically understand it, is unstructured and should be treated as the child's personal time, it is also often structured by the children themselves for it is a serious matter from the perspective of the child (Ramstetter & Murray, 2017). Given this, teacher intervention in students' play should only occur, a la Rousseau's negative ideal, for reasons of safety or when some students interfere with the play of others. A particular student's play (or that of groups of students playing together) at a particular activity might carry on for minutes, hours, or even days. This is natural. Therefore, if schools are to continue to play a role in supporting children's development, they might better do so as democratic play environments that empower students to pursue their interests as well as their integration (Rolstad, 2012). This will require educators to rethink "learning" as a form of structured play. Children can play with lots of things, including ideas and dreams. But they must be exposed to them and such exposure should happen not only from book learning but engagement with and, especially, for people.

Unschooling as Critical CSL

Getting students out of schools by making them radically public is an important way of disengaging the structures of fixity. As I noted, Illich's notion of deschooling (which, for convenience, I have been using interchangeably with unschooling) was based on the idea of getting students face-to-face with people out of schools through what he referred to as learning webs. As I have emphasized, Illich never addressed the problem of how those things he found being so reprehensibly reproduced in schools might be reproduced out of schools as well. Therefore, the idea of unschooling I have in mind becomes a critically oriented pedagogical variant within Illich's learning webs through critically directed service learning. Critical service learning requires reflection toward solving material problems in context and engages a space for education as enacted social justice.

From this orientation, we might think of unschooling as a progression of Rousseau's aleatory materialism, at least as Althusser interprets and builds on it. Sotiris' (2014) take here is worth citing at some length:

> Althusser's reading of Rousseau's state of pure nature as an origin that is separated by whatever follows, offers an opportunity to think the new emphasis on the encounter and more generally a more aleatory conception of social reality. For this conception it is important not only to view social relations as encounters—and not as essential connections—but also to present the very possibility of non-lasting encounters, of encounters that do not create social relations and social forms. In this sense, the forest, as the space that is not place, the space that represents the void that is necessary for this interplay of encounters, is one of the most forceful images that Althusser finds in order to think this empty space of—in the last instance—political practice. (p.13)

I think we might reconceive of Illich's learning webs and even Sheffield's radical CSL, both of which place emphasis on the encounter, as taking place in the void. As Sotiris (2014) continues,

> It does not matter that the forest is in reality full, of trees, of animals, of human beings. It is empty and void in the same sense that the Italian conjuncture for Machiavelli was empty, namely it was lacking the constitutive political intervention (or the constitutive accident) that would initiate a sequence of new encounters, of the encounters that could last and consequently of new social and political configurations. (p. 13)

Learning webs certainly, and to a lesser degree service learning, present non-lasting encounters. Even so, the materialism of the encounter is lasting. This, in turn, allows the encounterer to enter the next encounter from an importantly different onto-epistemic space. This includes the encounter with the school and, thus, we can begin to reimagine schools as without walls.

Here, however, we must be cautious about how we create the encounter. As with any attempt to unfix education, service learning takes on a number of definitions and can even be predatory. To the extent, for example, that service learning requirements are set up as one-time, course-completing events, they essentially treat community agencies and their constituents as curricular fodder such that students can tick a box and get a grade. Here, student experience is privileged over all else and wholly represented via the grade. This shapes service learning much like the community service that is meted out by systems of jurisprudence as a punishment. Similarly, educators confuse philanthropy, volunteerism, or charity as forms of community service. Such forms of community service are unidirectional—"we're here to help you"—and tend to have effects antithetical to both democracy and transformation. Such forms of so-called service learning simply do not provide a critical experience, serving instead as an extension of existing bureaucracy.

What is required instead is a radicalized or critical understanding of CSL which pays particular attention to how such an approach to education might reengage with the public spaces in which schooling exists. The goal is to get students out of school such that those experiences, those encounters, count in school and help us to reimagine schools as radically public spaces that rely on other public spaces for their full functioning. Again, Sheffield (2011) begins the development of this ideal with his notion of "strong community service learning." Further, Sheffield is careful to displace "service learning" with "*community* service learning." It is important to note here that schools themselves are not only embryonic communities, as Dewey describes them, but also integral (or should be integral) to the larger community. Contrary to Illich, this claim entails the importance of schools in an institutional sense. The opposite—that the larger community is integral to the school—is also true and crucial to the ideal of unschooling in schools. Thus extends the previous assertion to the "right to the school" as a challenge to the existing neoliberal order. An understanding of service learning as community-based is crucial to the possibility of education for democracy and guides its transformative potential. This strong sense of community (in the simultaneously socio-spatial sense) remains a missing element in notions of unschooling, even as constant association with others is key to understandings of unschooling.

Sheffield begins with the understanding that a contemporary purpose of CSL is to reinvigorate democratic habits of mind. Engagement in CSL should include active and informed participation in society, incorporating a civic view of service. Here reflective thinking is a key dispositional aim of CSL for the advancement of habits of thought necessary to democracy. Among other things, this is derivative of the necessity of interacting with other community members, usually "strangers," viewed as equal partners in the democratic project, regardless of difference.

While the advancement of democratic habits of mind—the development of which requires attending to the tenets of liberalism outlined in Chapter 1—is certainly a noble and necessary goal, Sheffield recognizes the material effects of contemporary approaches to CSL, casting them as a "weaker" form of schooling. Though some versions of CSL are seemingly oriented from a social justice perspective, they remain problematic as they seek to develop in students an *appreciation* of issues such as homelessness, poverty, the lack of a living wage, etc., yet never fully engage within the material contexts of such injustice. Much like predatory models, even social justice-oriented service learning can become voyeuristic to the extent that in order to gain an appreciation of homelessness and the plight of the homeless, for example, service learners enter the shelter, distribute food, count the homeless, and move on; the "space" of homelessness remains an external deviation through which students pass on their way toward an evaluative grade. Consider what kinds of questions reflection on such an experience might entail: Where do "they" gather? How many homeless people are there in our city, county, municipality...? The actions to which such questions lead are simply more of the same: counting the number of homeless, doing a food collection, volunteering occasionally to distribute food, etc. Notice how, much like the example from a previous chapter of how soda machines reveal the illusion of autonomy, the experiences from this kind of service learning also reproduce the illusion of autonomy while simultaneously pretending to be something radical.

Such experiences and reflection ultimately serve to get well-meaning people off the hook; they remain materially disengaged from the issues they seek to address. By focusing on the where and the how many, we can do our "good" and move on. In so doing, we not only miss but can also ignore the truly critical question: Why are people homeless? What are the structural causes of homelessness which we all participate in and support (consciously or not)? How might the above actions (of counting, collecting, etc.) make us complicit in the very hegemonic rationale we perhaps seek to subvert? Notice that such questions refuse the "responsibilized" individualism that Vassallo earlier questioned as an effect of self-regulated learning.

"Strong" CSL, then, can be achieved by recognizing, as with critical pedagogy, the "critical" roots of CSL wherein critical reflection, especially as it is applied to a real problem, becomes the dispositional aim. This requires not only reflective thinking, the core of democratic practice, but also "critical reflection on systematically oppressive institutional structures" (Sheffield, 2011, p. 45). Such reflection is engendered by mutuality—an understanding that "your" cause is mine and there is mutual benefit in working together to engage it—and solidarity. As Sheffield puts it, "solidarity develops into a disposition toward democratic interaction and service. It is a readiness to act, to respond to the stranger. It answers [the] demand that projects...dispose the individual to future such experiences" (p. 82). Solidarity invokes relational thinking—that we are never fully external to the structures or contexts we seek to change. Note that solidarity results in a readiness to act not just in any way but in ways driven by critical reflection. In this sense, Sheffield's notion of solidarity as a necessary component of critical schooling not only aligns with Soja's demand for a relational orientation in the name of spatial justice but also understands Althusser's aleatory materialism.

Building from the discussion of critical pedagogy, the role of the teacher within the formal institutional space of school in CSL is to prepare students for the material experience (reading and learning about who, what, where), to provide the academic tools necessary to understanding and seeking solutions to a given empirical situation, and to provide constructive opportunities for reflection upon the experience (the critical why) both in and out of schools. Notice that undertaking the learning of such skills should be driven largely by interest in the empirical situation. Reflection is continuous, before, during, and after any service experience—it is not limited to a fixed space (wherein the confected, and static, space of homelessness, for example, remains the *object* of reflection). Reflection requires transaction, in that the subject not only knows the object differently but the self differently as well. Indeed, in the example of homelessness, the transaction must now be one between subjects as it is revealing of social space and relations. In this sense, CSL dwells in the relational space of the socio-spatial dialectic, doing so with the intention of bringing about some element of change.

What is key here is the emotional disequilibrium that the CSL project, now a lived experience, evokes. It is such disequilibrium that results in psychic transformation that drives the communal transformative potential found in acting to recover that equilibrium (Sheffield, 2015). In this way, the CSL project becomes a felt problem, one that is not imposed from the outside but one that gains its power from the interest and care of the learner herself. In short, the very material experience of CSL makes possible a productive affect, one that requires a necessary reorientation within the educational moment.

But if it is emotional disequilibrium that evokes this interest in the first place, especially vis-à-vis socially just communal transformation, what sparks the emotional disequilibrium? This is what Dewey refers to as a "hitch": "incompatible factors within the empirical situation" wherein "opposed responses are provoked which cannot be taken simultaneously in overt action" (Dewey, 1916, pp. 10–11). Such tensions are to some degree emotionally laden which, for Dewey, is the catalyst for thought and reflection. This is, in fact, the "transaction" that I referred to earlier. As Petrovic and Rosiek (2003) discuss it, the hitch or disequilibrium requires the subject

> to reflect on the tension that such hitches create and devise a way to cope with it. This coping requires the modification of both the subject and object of study. In this transaction, the object acquires new meaning for the subject and any time a subject reconstructs the object of her inquiry she also is changed. For she now "knows" in an altered way, and this new knowing must be made consistent with the other habits that constitute the self. (p. 162)

There remains a constructive parallel here between Dewey's "hitch" and Soja's belief in the socio-spatial dialectic as a means for creating new ways of thinking and being that are not predetermined by governing norms. Both conceptualizations of learning point to an inherent tension between understanding "what was" and "what possibly could be." In this connection, disequilibrium becomes an embodied dialectic, a movement from within sparked by the materialism of the encounter. As Young (2011) notes,

> people will be motivated to reflect on themselves and their relations with others only in concrete social circumstances of cooperation where they recognize problems—the political group in which gays and lesbians voice dissatisfaction, the company that never seems to promote women and therefore loses them, the school or neighborhood with racial conflict. (p. 155)

Coping with the tension such cooperation engenders requires the modification of both the subject and object of study. In this transaction the object acquires new meaning for the subject and anytime a subject reconstructs the object of her inquiry she is also changed and education is unfixed as dialectical engagement, as per the discussion of the hitch above. However, notice that the object of study, now known differently, is, in the case of radicalized CSL, the unjust empirical situation. Having yet to be transformed, the unjust material situation maintains the emotional disequilibrium and, thus, provokes action. It is for this reason that CSL theory and experience must "incorporate the deeply difficult or the terribly tragic fact of human experience" (Sheffield, 2015, p. 50). The space of CSL remains unfixed, the educational moment unhinged from assumed principles of stasis. When considered within the material space of education, CSL makes possible a vision of schools as radically public, a space that refuses to be fixed along neoliberal norms.

In other words, radical CSL seeks to unfix education, destabilizing students through emotional disequilibrium toward action even as it usefully disrupts the stilting spatial binary of education within schools and not without. Combined with the application of traditional academic learning to real problems, CSL draws from a radically public sense of education to reanimate possibility. As alluded to in the discussion of critical pedagogy, for this to happen, schools must not engage in practices that run counter to the ideal of radical service learning and its democratic animation (e.g., tracking). At a minimum, students must engage such ideas academically. This must be an ongoing refusal to allow schools to remain closed, static spaces and ongoing engagement with the structures of fixity that can only undermine movement to the democratic habits of thought necessary for engagement in radical CSL.

Conclusion

In this day and age, we are forced to recognize basic issues of safety. However, our fear contributes to fixing our schools. The current and increasing geography of schools is one that evinces a lockdown, one that fixes the boundaries that separate schools from the communities of which they are a part. This is just one of many challenges critical pedagogues face to unfix schools. So what does the unfixed school—school now as unschooling in school combined with unschooling out of school—require? Here are some central conclusions:

1. Critical pedagogy must engage with and build on a philosophy of unschooling in school and its implications. This is, in many respects, a matter of depth. While certainly required, critical pedagogy cannot only inform the ways teachers approach the traditional curriculum, creating the capacity for perspective taking and critical thinking through a problem-posing education. This is where many so-called critical pedagogues stop. As I suggested in Chapter 3, it is here that thinking critically can become necrophilic and devolve into a simple form of

know-how. Critical pedagogy must be aimed at social transformation, especially against the inequality that is a natural by-product of capitalism. Of course, this too can occur through traditional engagement with subject-area content and the kinds of questions critical pedagogues ask of and about that content. But, a philosophy of unschooling in school requires critical pedagogues to take the material reality of schools seriously and to engage with it. This, too, is a matter of depth. Students can and should analyze their schools, like Marxist reproduction theorists, and come to understand how schools are reproductive of extant and unjust social relations and the dominant ideology. But teachers and students must also engage as (neo)Marxian resistance theorists and seek to change, in schools, the material conditions that provide the foundation for such reproduction. The philosophy of unschooling in school highlights many of these conditions.

2. Apropos to the first point, and at the risk of belaboring the point, one of the material conditions that is again relevant here is the corporate mentality of accountability which manifests as grades in schools. Children should not be fixated on or fixed by grades or tests. Grades fix children into unhealthy academic categories. Educators and parents tend to grade and to grade a lot. Educators, parents, and certainly policy makers have come to expect grades. And, in so doing, we get motivation wrong. We misunderstand the learning process. We change learning from play to work, working for pay in the form of a grade. Just as Rousseau presented the education of Emile through different stages, in the early stages, in order to make schooling more like unschooling, there should be no grades, no tests, no assessments beyond teacher observation and the learning creations of the students.

3. Play also requires freedom of movement and communication. All too often, students are disciplined into docility—a passive formation of learning that rewards fixity. In this sense, "good" students are often those recognized as the least disruptive and, of course, this extends to the material realities of schooling. "Good" students take up the least amount of space, performing a docile independence that requires little of teachers and administrators alike. But students have a right to a different school, to a materially different engagement in education. This requires refusing the fixity that has plagued contemporary educational reform in favor of a radically public school—one that exists in

dialectical relation with communities specifically, and the larger citizenry more generally, and brings the aliveness and movement of the community to the classroom.

4. Therefore, children should, in school, engage with a variety of community members, *a lot*: electricians, cooks, plumbers, politicians, mothers, fathers, and maybe even philosophers. And children should be in the community, *a lot*. Certainly, Illich's notion of learning webs remains important and part of what I am supporting. This could also include traditional field trips, which are especially important to underprivileged students. Importantly, however, I have suggested that engagement with the community must be given critical direction. That is to say, just as unschooling in school requires critical pedagogues to resist the reproductive material conditions within schools, unschooling requires critical pedagogues to understand and resist the material conditions out of school. I have suggested radical CSL as a way to engage criticality outside of schools.

On this point, Sheffield's CSL could provide even more critical direction by incorporating—not that it explicitly excludes it—something like environmental justice pedagogy. In his discussion of educating for earth consciousness, Toro (2016) observes, "The great challenge of walking towards more respectful and balanced livelihoods with nature is that humans must come to understand ourselves in a holistic and integrative sense" (p. 213). I think this is another link to the spirit of a Marxian orientation. Through environmental justice pedagogy, the general sense of equality that Marxism engenders is enhanced.

Furthermore, environmental issues entail complex social and economic issues. They do so, as Boxley (2017) notes, "at multiple geographical scales so that students can empirically locate themselves within them and develop critical, historical and transformative knowledge" (p. 72). Importantly, such work engages all subject matter: most obviously health, geography, and history and how development has created environmental problems. Climate change requires mathematics and measurement. The consideration of issues of public and open space requires politics and philosophy. Questions of sustainable transport delve into engineering and physics. This points to the increasing need for "green curricula." This is, in fact, a new area of concern in chemistry (Lasker, Mellor, Mullins, Nesmith,

& Simcox, 2017). Green chemistry involves "the design of chemical products and processes that reduce or eliminate the use or generation of hazardous substances" (p. 984).

If we are to situate education as a means toward productive social change, we need a radical reconfiguration of the spatial properties of schooling as well as the discursive ways we orient activities within different spaces. CSL, especially now as informed by environmental justice pedagogy, helps to reveal the ethico-political implications of this shift. Students come to experience their lives as entangled with others and questions, like homelessness, as something other than dead abstractions. In this way, again, even nonlasting encounters create a sense of relationality and solidarity. The encounter then engenders real disequilibrium that can be tackled in subject matter in school, creating its own aliveness. Students should then be flooded with the resources to engage their disequilibrium, which, because no longer connected to an abstraction and, thus, of real interest, becomes more like play. Such resources should be those seen in the community and presented by community members. Notice here, and throughout, it is the tutor's responsibility to design and set up such floods in the classroom, or, whenever possible, bring children to where these resources already exist. Play is important philosophically and discursively. Approaching learning discursively as "work" surely engenders other work-ish (neoliberal) ways and approaches teachers take.

Mapping contemporary realities of education can prove overwhelming. The dominating extension of neoliberal norms into the daily practices of schooling (and living) seems to cover nearly all points of resistance, appropriating even well-intentioned attempts at social change into normative processes of fixity. Yet, critical pedagogues maintain a commitment to alternative means for education and situate schools as avenues toward social justice. If we take seriously the socio-spatial dialectic in which schools are produced, change is possible. Indeed, Jean Anyon (2011) began to recognize the need for education to operate in excess of traditional school boundaries and within local communities:

> We need to move our work beyond the classroom walls into the worlds in which low-income, black and Latino, and immigrant students live. We can…involve our students in contestation in public places—public struggles over rights, injustice, and opportunity. (p. 97)

Anyon's advocacy points to a need to move outside of the classroom space. But this must also recognize the importance of such educational spaces. Indeed, to move "beyond the classroom walls" is to, dialectically speaking, simultaneously change the classroom walls themselves. It is to animate educational spaces as more than static containers for fixing students. It is to pursue unschooling in school; critical pedagogues create the swerve. In other words, animating traditional education spaces requires not only taking the inside out, as Anyon suggests, but also bringing the outside in. Unschooling, in its turn, must require that students be encouraged to take on public struggles in public places as part of their education. Further, educators and community members must join these students in such public contestation as a necessary element of schooling. Unschooling in school combined with unschooling creates a dialectic that opens a space in which the radically public school might take hold.

The radically public school, as Sheffield suggested, engages the tragic fact of human experience. At first blush, this might suggest that the radically public school must be intended for those students who have not faced the daily tragic. It is they for whom the swerve is necessary. But, the swerve obtains nonetheless in facing one's existence, even a tragic one. In a study on students living in generational poverty (Beegle, 2003), participants noted the shame they felt over the lack of control they had over their lives, embarrassment over their own appearance or that of family members, and humiliation over the kind of lunch they had to bring to school (e.g., "tea in a mayonnaise jar"). They felt disconnected from school and from teachers who seemed to not care about their experience. Clearly, these students experience the very things that we expect students from privileged backgrounds to come to understand and experience (albeit differently and to lesser degree) through things like critical pedagogy and radical CSL. Nevertheless, Beegle, in a crucial observation, points out that her participants "felt that understanding root causes of poverty was instrumental in shedding the false burden of responsibility for the social condition of their youth" (p. 17). Shedding this is the first step toward empowerment, agency, and subjecthood. It is the aperture of the wide-awakeness of Maxine Greene and the conscientization of Paolo Freire. It is the realization of one's material conditions and the revelation of how Althusser's ideological interpellation functions. It is the process, instead, of calling oneself into being through the enactment of one's (limited) freedom which grows alongside the capacity for autonomy. This is the hope of the radically public, unfixed school.

Notes

1. This analysis owes largely to Kuntz and Petrovic (2018).
2. This quote came originally from unschooling.com (now a defunct website). It seems to be a ubiquitous definition that can be found on numerous unschooling, deschooling and homeschooling sites. More recently, it appears at https://prezi.com/rdl_aeupjt4q/the-concept-of-unschooling/.
3. Anyon specifies "low-income students of color" in her quote. But I think such activism will benefit all students. For information on the history of the Mexican-American studies program, see McGinnis (2011).

· 6 ·

AUTHENTICITY, IDENTITY POLITICS, AND CRITICAL PEDAGOGY

In Chapter 3, I briefly raised the notion of existential authenticity and argued that while it is also imperative to justice to recognize and deal with other concerns of existential authenticity, this should not distract the left from its Marxist roots and the structural centrality of social class and the pernicious effects of capitalist social relations. This chapter represents a bit of a sidebar to anticipate reaction to this position. Here I want to revisit that discussion and argue, on the one hand, that one such distraction has been the rise of identity politics. I think Boxley is correct in his assertion that "Whilst children are actively taught—sometimes and in some schools—to challenge racism, homophobia, sexism, transphobia, they are nowhere taught to challenge the logic of capitalism" (p. 111). Part of the reason for this is that logic of capitalism has become simply logic. I have provided many examples of how this permeates schools as commonsensically good teaching. The point of this chapter is to provide, drawing mainly on the 2016 US Presidential election, an analysis of identity politics, its dangers, and its necessity.

Contrary to Boxley's position, there is also something important to the observation made by Springer, Lopes de Souza, and White (2016) that "a purely Marxian take leaves us with significant blind spots that cannot be reconciled within the econocentric lens of Marxism" (p. 2). Even as, as I have argued, a Marxian approach leads to a greater sense of equality generally that brings into relief other forms of oppression, it would be a mistake to dismiss the importance of identity politics or politics of difference. As Sonia Nieto (1999) has noted, "The insistence that students must be involved in the process of their own education, a central tenet of critical pedagogy, has inspired the inclusion of student voices that had heretofore been missing from most treatments of multicultural education" (p. 179). So, there is certainly a need for identity politics to inform critical pedagogy to help create the relief mentioned. Still, I maintain that the Marxist tradition is the necessary foundation here. Thus, I take the driving question of Young's (2011) project to develop a politics of difference at face value: "How can traditional socialist appeals to equality and democracy be *deepened* and *broadened* as a result of [the group-based social movements such as feminism, Black liberation, and gay and lesbian rights]?" (p. 3, emphasis added).

Identity and Group-Based Politics

At its best, I think identity politics directly reflects the raison d'etre of critical pedagogy as a mode of consciousness-raising about the contradictions of complex social systems, (especially, given the focus of this project, capitalist ones) and seeking to overcome the differential effects this has on different groups of people. Identity politics makes explicit that such examinations must include the lived circumstances of historically marginalized groups and ultimately requires taking political action to change those circumstances. Some of these circumstances certainly trace back to capitalist social relations. As regards racism, for example, McLaren and Muñoz (2000) have argued that "Whiteness is a sociohistorical form of consciousness, born at the nexus of capitalism colonial rule, and the emergent relationships among dominant and subordinate groups" (p. 40). Similarly, the feminization of teaching resulted from sexism and the exclusion of women from commerce and male professions. Furthermore, as Strober and Tyack (1980) note, "Advocates of women as teachers, such as Catharine Beecher, Mary Lyon, Zilpah Grant, Horace Mann, and Henry Barnard, worked hard to create private and public normal schools to train young women for their divinely designated profession, thereby publicizing their virtues *as well as their cheapness*" (p. 496, emphasis added).

Of course, not all instances of oppression can trace back to capitalism. When teachers are put on leave, as happened recently in Texas (Platoff, 2018), for "promoting the homosexual agenda," this has nothing to do with capitalism. Yet, it has as much to do with social justice as economic inequality. For social justice, as Papageorgiou (1980) takes it, "implies, among other things, equality of the burdens, the advantages, and the opportunities of citizenship" (p. 110). Clearly, social justice does not reign in some Texas school districts. Of course, in the United States, there are a number of states with what have been referred to as "no homo promo" laws.

In the United States, identity politics, although not described as such at the time, begins in the 1960s with the civil rights movement. Of course, the civil rights movement is not too distant from the ethnic movements that have always been part and parcel of American politics. Eric Hobsbawm (1996) argues that what he referred to as "the new ethnicity" "makes its first public appearance with Glazer and Moynihan's *Beyond the Melting Pot* in 1963 and becomes a militant programme with Michael Novak's *The Rise of the Unmeltable Ethnics* in 1972" (p. 39). The new ethnicity was followed by the gay and lesbian liberation movement, continuing through the women's liberation movement of the 1980s. Of course, the women's liberation movement did not necessarily speak to the issues of black women (hence the emergence of black feminist thought). Nevertheless, such strategic essentialism (as Spivak termed it) is necessary to identity politics. Thus, Young (2011) argues that in order to deepen traditional socialist appeals, "a conception of justice should begin with the concepts of domination and oppression" and that "where social group differences exist and some groups are privileged while others are oppressed, social justice requires explicitly acknowledging and attending to those group differences in order to undermine oppression" (p. 3). Here Young urges a shift away from justice as a problem of distribution, a la some egalitarian projects such as that of John Rawls. But, again, I took, and still take, Young's original question as written even as her own position now seems not to. To my mind, the overriding injustice remains distribution, analyses of which have provided many of the conceptual tools—hegemony, ideology, exploitation, etc.—to understanding other important forms of oppression. In this way, even as it is a mistake to reduce all oppression to capitalism, Young is correct to observe that "the oppressions experienced by many members of [oppressed groups] are certainly conditioned by the specific structures and imperatives of American capitalism" (p. 122). With this foundational understanding in mind, it is the case that both identity and class politics are necessary and unstable.

Identity or Class Politics

Identity politics played out quite starkly in the 2016 US Presidential elections, mainly in the form of critiques, from both the left and right, against the strategy of Hilary Clinton. From Clinton's political left arose a class solidarity argument. Historically, the Democratic Party had the full support of the unions (and still largely does) and many middle-/working-class people tended democratic, even when more socially conservative. However, in the 2016 election Clinton only carried the union household vote by 8% over Trump, an historic low. Thus, her democratic primary opponent, Senator Bernie Sanders, warned that the Democratic Party's future rests on whether it can "go beyond identity politics." He went on to say that he was "deeply humiliated" by the party's failure to attract more people with *his* white, working-class background. Sanders is not the first to provide this critique. This was also a complaint of Hobsbawm and others. Indeed, Edward Luttwak, in "The endangered American Dream," seems absolutely prophetic on this count:

> Members of labor unions, and unorganized unskilled workers, will sooner or later realize that their government is not even trying to prevent wages from sinking or to prevent jobs from being exported. Around the same time, they will realize that suburban white-collar workers—themselves desperately afraid of being downsized—are not going to let themselves be taxed to provide social benefits for anyone else. At that point, something will crack. The nonsuburban electorate will decide that the system has failed and start looking around for a strongman to vote for—someone willing to assure them that, once he is elected, the smug bureaucrats, tricky lawyers, overpaid bond salesmen, and postmodernist professors will no longer be calling the shots … One thing that is very likely to happen is that the gain made in the past forty years by black and brown Americans, and by homosexuals, will be wiped out. Jocular contempt for women will come back into fashion … All the resentment which badly educated Americans feel about having their manners dictated to them by college graduates will find an outlet.

While certainly not a strong man by typical measures of decency, honesty, or ethics, Donald Trump clearly fits this bill of strongman.

More importantly, here again, we see the importance of beginning from a Marxist perspective. For it is quite clear that the government is "not even trying to prevent wages from sinking." Indeed, neoliberalism and the neoliberal policy-making that has taken hold in the United States demonstrate the structural interdependence of so-called free markets and the state. This has been the modus operandi since the conservative revolution of Ronald

Reagan in 1980. The Reagan revolution largely ushered in neoliberalism (think trickle-down economics) but was supported by neoconservatives (conservatives or paleo-conservatives are now largely extinct in the US political system) and joined by authoritarian populists (the radical evangelical right).

The Economic Policy Institute notes that "in the three decades following World War II, hourly compensation of the vast majority of workers rose 91 percent, roughly in line with productivity growth of 97 percent. But for most of the past generation (except for a brief period in the late 1990s), pay for the vast majority lagged further and further behind overall productivity. From 1973 to 2013, hourly compensation of a typical (production/nonsupervisory) worker rose just 9 percent while productivity increased 74 percent." The Institute also points out, "the extraordinarily rapid growth of annual wages for the top 1 percent compared with everybody else: Top 1 percent wages grew 138 percent, while wages of the bottom 90 percent grew just 15 percent." In other words, there is precious little "trickle down."

One of the reasons for this is the financialization of the economy (Anyon, 2011). Increasingly, large corporations make money not through production and investment in the real economy but through money, in financial speculation. There has been a direct correlation between government-supported deregulation and the rise of profits from speculation.[1] In the 1960s, profits from speculation were about 15% of all profits of all companies. Today it is more like 50%. So, on the one hand, the working class is an increasingly oppressed group in the United States against whom the deck is stacked, as Sanders rightly asserts.

On the other hand, class politics (the political right dismisses this as class warfare)—even as a form of identity politics—is no longer capable of creating or maintaining the base that democrats once held. Ideological hegemony functions quite powerfully here. For example, when Governor Bob Riley (R) stunned his party by introducing a progressive tax plan for Alabama in 2003, polls indicated that low to middle income voters—those who would have benefited most—opposed the plan by 30%, a margin far higher than opposition from upper income voters. Of course, a vigorous, expensive, and misleading propaganda blitz came from opponents, and that is likely to have had an impact. Arguably, however, the narratives of big (bad) government and rugged individualism are likely to have played a strong part in the ultimate defeat of the plan. Ideas function ideologically when they help to reproduce unjust relations, domination, or oppression (Young, 2011).

There is also a history of low-income white voters siding with the plantocracy in the south. So the question of whether or not white voters tend to vote against their own interests raises its head again. This is not at all clear if the interests continue to include the "psychological wages" and white privileges of white supremacy, as DuBois argued in *Black Reconstruction*. In the United States, we have witnessed that when political work is done to counter a history of racism, a white backlash awaits. Thus, after decades of progress in civil rights, we witnessed the Reagan Revolution. Ronald Reagan opposed the civil rights movement, the women's equality movement, the gay and lesbian liberation movement, and he attacked student protesters of the Vietnam War as "not having a right to an education." The election of Donald Trump seems a similar kind of backlash against President Obama who, according to many if not most Trump voters, practiced "reverse racism" and increased the racial divide. As far as I can tell, he did this by calling attention to injustices against the black community. In response, Trump, in his ghastly rhetoric, set up white voters to consider the evils of "the other" over their own economic interests. And they did. Thus, it is not surprising that the coalitions that Clinton and Trump put together, each its own brand of identity politics, included Clinton receiving the votes of 88% of African Americans and Trump getting the votes of 63% of white men and a majority (52%) of white women (despite his misogyny).

So identity politics held far more sway than class politics in the final election results and were engaged by both sides. For the left, it was a strategic catastrophe. Perhaps Sanders foresaw that, engaging, instead, in a class solidarity campaign. Of course, it was not merely a strategic decision but a position and philosophy he has held consistently throughout his political career.

Problematically, however, we—even like-minded democratic socialists—should be concerned that Sanders' direction, a class politics, can become a kind of apologetics to the extent that class solidarity justifies overlooking intersectionality, and differentiated forms of injustice. The comedian, Bill Maher, concluded, for example, that the Democratic Party failed because its leaders "made white people feel like a minority." This is some kind of bizarre left twist on political correctness: I am sorry you got your feelings hurt, white man. Trump voters told pollsters that "diversity comes at the expense of whites" and that the federal government, throughout American history, has provided too much assistance to black citizens. In the end, there is much truth to columnist David Masciotra's (2017) conclusion that "The crucial aim of American politics, according to the increasingly widespread view of opposition to 'identity politics,' is to make white cowards and bigots feel that they have no need for growth, and that they are the center of the universe" (para. 5). So, Clinton supporters can legitimately say to Sanders' supporters that the fact that a large number of racists voted for a racist is not Clinton's fault. And while white liberals might have been surprised by Trump's election, I am reasonably sure that most black voters were not. Apropos to this, two-thirds of Trump supporters still believe President Obama is Muslim; 40% believe that blacks are lazier than whites; a third believe that homosexuals should be banned from entering the country; and 20% disagreed with the Emancipation Proclamation! (Legum, 2016).

Right Identity Politics

Rightists dismiss identity politics as just so much political correctness. Their critiques, while lacking the important class analysis that Sanders provides, still sound very much like the critiques from the left: "No one seems to have a satisfying definition of what 'identity politics' means, exactly, but the message is clear: Liberals have been paying too much attention to race and gender and sexual orientation—or not enough attention to the right variants of those—and sensible Americans are rightly saying 'no thanks.'" "American liberalism," writes Columbia historian Mark Lilla (2016), "has slipped into a kind of moral panic about racial, gender, and sexual identity that has distorted liberalism's message and prevented it from becoming a unifying force capable of governing" (para. 2).

Glick and Keller (2016) argue that "Political correctness has reached a point where it is essentially impossible to have an honest, open conversation about sensitive issues. Trump's rise is nothing more than a direct response to the growing trend of language policing" and that "Every time a social justice warrior tries to call out Donald Trump over supposed bigotry, he, she, they, or ze adds more fuel to the Trump fire" (para. 8). So, if identity politics is *a mode of consciousness-raising about the lived circumstances of historically marginalized groups* and *taking political action to change those circumstances*, then the first part of the definition is simply dismissed as political correctness.

On the one hand, political correctness does have some negative effects, including, in fact, making people afraid or, at least, trepidatious about entering conversations about important issues, especially those dealing with oppression. How can you talk about race, for example, if you are not sure if you can say "black" or if you should say "African American," while also acknowledging that not all black people are African American. I think there are legitimate concerns here. On the other hand, it is probably a good thing when people might actually feel a need to stop to think about how others might like to be recognized. But that is a bridge too far for the right. What is missing, and this was the discourse that took hold in the Trump campaign, is people "telling it like it is." During the election, a friend of mine suggested, "We can't be candid anymore." So the antidote to political correctness is "candor." Below are presented several common defenses of "candor" that surfaced during Trump's rise:

Debi Lee 1/20/2017 7:12 AM CST And that's the irony of the left who claim to be the so very tolerant, "treat everyone EQUAL." Rather than being ever so sensitive to insulting a woman (WHY??? We're SUPPOSE to be equal to men, I say, if we are equal, we must take the good with the bad) Trump is ACTUALLY demonstrating COMPLETELY EQUAL TREATMENT, REGARDLESS WHO THE PERSON IS.	Donald J. Trump ✔ @realDonaldTrump At least 7 dead and 48 wounded in terror attack and Mayor of London says there is "no reason to be alarmed!"We must stop being politically correct and get down to the business of security for our people. If we don't get smart it will only get worse
Nic Tanney Idpositive 1/6/2016 6:58 AM CST Ever since this PC crap all started it was designed to be the true harbinger of anti-america leftists leaning idiots who would not or could not debate the good of it. Shame on all you stupid people for ruining this great country.	jc11choate 1/6/2016 1:26 PM CST Trump brings out what the Silent Majority has been thinking for the last 7 years but is to afraid to say it, because of all the tree huggers and do gooders in the Democratic Party and all those that think in the same way. It's great to have someone finally say it like it is, rather than every single word and speech that has been run through a sieve to make sure all of the offensive comments that may be harmful to someone or some nationality have been deleted!

Here we see a critical lack of self-reflection. This same friend who raised the issue of candor is also a National Guardsman recently deployed to the Middle East. I wonder what the response might be if I welcomed him back by saying something like, "So, how did the oil protection business go?" I can tell you that this would cause quite a stir in many circles, even among liberal circles, as disrespectful. We want to think our service men and women are doing something far more noble: They are protecting our freedom. To suggest that they are doing anything other, even unknowingly, is, well, "deplorable." Similarly, after 9/11 it was impossible to have a conversation about "why?" A question like "why do they hate us?" received a fairly pat answer: "They are jealous of our freedom." "The only good Muslim is a dead Muslim." But asking something a bit more self-reflective like, "What about our history of relations with the Middle East might have led to such resentment?" Such a question invariably generated the response "You're just one of those blame America first liberals." Questioning American exceptionalism is taboo. Now, the irony that all of this is just a form of political correctness seems to escape most conservatives. But that is what it is. More accurately, perhaps, it is what Henry Giroux (2007) refers to as patriotic correctness: Patriotic correctness is an unreflective, unnuanced, full-throated defense of American exceptionalism, nationalism, historical revision, and cherry-picked myths, ideals, and heroes. Where political correctness may hinder conversation, it is not overtly dangerous. Patriotic correctness, however, is. This is perhaps best captured in a very popular country song by Toby Keith:

> Hey, Uncle Sam put your name at the top of his list
> And the Statue of Liberty started shakin' her fist
> And the eagle will fly man, it's gonna be hell
> When you hear mother freedom start ringin' her bell
> And it feels like the whole wide world is raining down on you
> Brought to you courtesy of the red white and blue
> Justice will be served and the battle will rage
> This big dog will fight when you rattle his cage
> And you'll be sorry that you messed with
> The U.S. of A.
> 'Cause we'll put a boot in your ass
> It's the American way

Now, in Keith's defense, this song came out right after 9/11 and I certainly understand the rage. However, this is not a momentary blip or venting. This is an ideology for much of the right in the United States. US politics has been driven by a politics of fear for some decades now, which has justified illegal military actions across the globe. At the risk of being accused of "blaming America first," here we might remember the lie of "weapons of mass destruction." Even more recently, Trump tossed around the idea of invading

Venezuela (Goodman, 2018) which would, of course, be a continuation of hostile and illegal US actions in that region (e.g., the overthrow of Salvador Allende in Chile, the installation of military dictatorship in Brazil, illegal military support of the Contras in Nicaragua, etc., etc.). It has also justified cutting social spending as the United States spends, by some accounts, more than the rest of the world combined on preparing for, waging, and cleaning up after such military action. In the meantime, while the United States voluntarily spends more of its GDP on the military than any other nation, Trump now complains that other nations need to do the same. Thus, the stakes in a global politics of fear get raised. So, patriotic correctness drives, at least in part, the dangerous identity politics of the right. But there are other features, mainly religious, as well.

Rod Dreher of the American Conservative begins an answer here. As he notes, "For some, racial and sexual identity politics matter more than theological truth."[2] He goes on to opine that "that is how the princess-and-the-pea mind of the Social Justice Warrior works. There is no more important cause in the world than eliminating all discrimination committed by hated demographic groups, while promoting discrimination by favored demographic groups." The "hated" demographic groups of the Trump coalition were white men, white Catholics, evangelicals, weekly churchgoers, and military personnel, a majority of whom voted for Trump.[3]

In short, it seems that the real problem is that whiteness, right-Christianity, straightness, and traditional masculinity are all forms of identity politics themselves. The opaqueness of this simple fact is constituted by layer upon layer, decade upon decade, of white supremacy. Trump clearly sought to exploit this as a form of identity politics as his campaign focused on black crime, illegal Latino immigration, and Muslim terrorists (starkly different from even his Republican predecessor). In other words, Trump overtly stoked the flames of a history of white supremacy that has required that our gaze be focused only on the other. In this topsy-turvy history, it is the other who is seen as oppositional. In fact, however, what we have witnessed historically is the active construction of the other, such that the dominant is born in opposition. Whiteness is not what it is, but what it is not. Such a process obscures the dominant as normalcy, the backdrop against which all else stands out. It is also related, then, to the way ideology also functions.

In Chapter 3, I noted how Michael Gove declared his nonideological space in UK policy-making. This process was similarly demonstrated in Senator Jeff Sessions' questioning of Sonia Sotomayor, then Supreme Court

Justice nominee. During confirmation hearings, Sessions questioned Sotomayor's ability to be objective and impartial because she is Latina. The very question, of course, betrays Sessions' own lack of impartiality as well as his belief in the myth of impartiality. The point is that Sessions' whiteness allows him to be everywhere while he can claim to be coming from nowhere, providing him the power to reinscribe hierarchy and oppression. That is to say, he need recognize no background that would lend to his being subjective or impartial. Sotomayor, in contrast, must claim to come from somewhere while being permitted to be nowhere.

Thus, on the one hand, Hobsbawm is correct to suggest that collective identities are defined negatively. On the other hand, I think this is much more the case for dominant than subordinate groups. Dominant groups share a taken-for-granted lived experience that, being largely institutionally unhampered, does not require them to reflect on that experience, whereas subordinate groups are required to inhabit a double situatedness or, to borrow from W. E. B. DuBois, a double consciousness. Thus, unlike the taken-for-grantedness of the dominant life, self-definition for subordinate groups comes from positive self-reflection. The challenge for the left, then, and critical pedagogues is how to make whiteness stand out against itself. This is particularly challenging when many whites and all right-Christians claim to be under attack. This is despite the fact that, depending on the poll, 75–85% of Americans identify as Christian, with only 4–5% claiming a non-Christian religion.

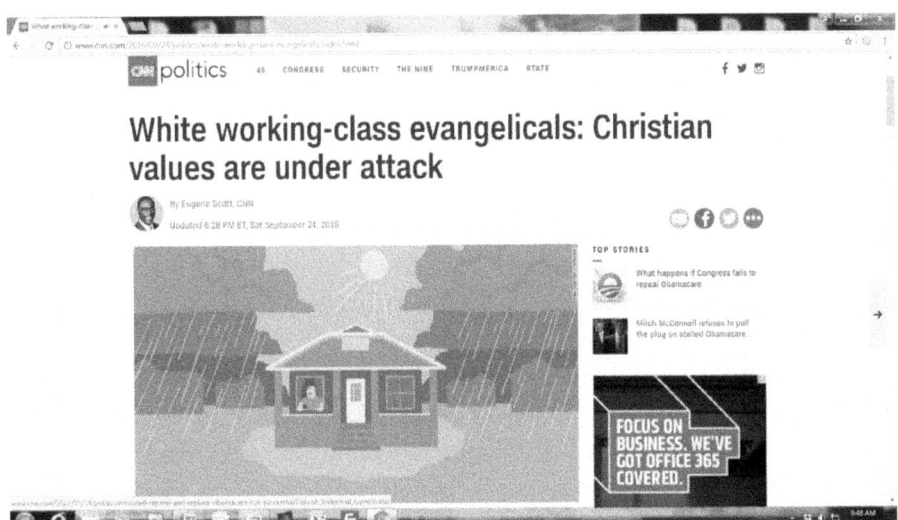

Conservative Christian claims of marginalization.

Focus on the Right with a Just Lens

So while the left divides itself because Clinton was unable to speak to the white working class; and Sanders was unable to speak to Clinton's minority coalition (black voters were simply not feeling the Bern), both must be engaged. On the one hand, the identity politics of the left is, I believe, morally right. On the other hand, it does involve a certain amount of myopia that, when it meets political strategy, is fatally flawed. In education, this myopia has led critical pedagogues too far away from their Marxist roots. But that does not mean that we should ignore what Trump voters allowed themselves to ignore or even support.

What Lilla and others keen on pulling the plug on conversations about multiculturalism and diversity don't realize is that by doing so, they play right into the hands of the newly emboldened neo-Nazis who helped put Trump in office and have delighted over several of his postelection staff and Cabinet picks. Shutting down these conversations, dismissing them as just so much political correctness—or perhaps more innocently redirecting them to the concerns of white, straight, mostly male Americans—is precisely what those groups want badly to see happen. This was what was behind the dangerously vocal backlash—the application of "candor"—that we are witnessing.

In advancing their own brand of identity politics, the alt-right, Christofascists, neo-Nazis, and even some relatively normal people in the Trump coalition had either to ignore or accept (and a majority praised) all of the following: Trump's grotesque rhetorical and physical assaults against women. As he said, after one debate "You could see there was blood coming out of her eyes, blood coming out of her wherever." Not long after this, he attacked a talk show host, as having begged to be invited to a Trump party, but he declined to invite her because "she was bleeding from a bad face job." Clearly, this is a pathological obsession with blood and women. Beyond this, of course, he has mocked the disabled. He is a racist who doesn't want "black guys" counting his money and thinks "laziness is a trait in blacks." And, begrudgingly, he assumes that "some" Mexicans are good people.

Given this, it is not hard to understand why Trump garnered the support of nationalist and white supremacist organizations. As written in the Crusader, "America was founded as a White Christian Republic. And as a White Christian Republic it became great" (Holley, 2016, para. 6). And, as David Duke (2016) pointed out, "Trump's attacks on Muslims and illegal immigration have brought his own beliefs into the mainstream" (para. 5). Rocky

Suhayda, chairman of the American Nazi Party, opined that Trump presents "a real opportunity" for them. "It doesn't have to be anti-, like the movement's been for decades, so much as it has to be pro-white," he added. Trump's disavowal of these specific endorsements rings quite hollow while alt-right crusader Steve Bannon served as an official advisor to the so-called president.

Implications for Educational Policy and Practice

On the one hand, Barack Obama was not much of a progressive when it came to educational policy. He kept largely intact and, in fact, exacerbated some of the worst neoliberal components of NCLB. His Race to the Top initiative imposed charter schools on states to seek federal funds. Trump's initial real moves in education policy (i.e., initiatives actually signed into law) are defensible even by progressives, including me. For example, the first resolution signed prevents the Department of Education from dictating prescriptive requirements for how states and school districts measure achievement. This at least provides the opportunity for states to move away from standardized exams. It is notable that students in US schools spend anywhere from 15 to 20% of a school year preparing for, taking, and resting from some standardized exam. Second, Trump rescinded part of the Higher Education Act having to do with teacher preparation. This regulation required states to issue annual ratings for training programs and these ratings were tied to the performance of teachers' students on standardized tests.

But identity politics is also important here and set a tone for both administrations. President Obama's focus was on the protection of minority students and closing the achievement gap through federal intervention. It was also about protecting minority students and women. For example, the Obama administration pushed schools to use alternatives to expelling or suspending students, since those punishments tend to affect black and Latino students more. In other words, the color-blind policies that occluded the disproportionate burden placed on students of color would no longer be tolerated. The Obama Administration also threatened to cut federal funding from a large number of universities that were under investigation for potentially violating federal antidiscrimination laws in the way they handled sexual assault claims (Perry Bacon, 2017).

Trump's focus is on states' rights and market intervention. With this combination, Trump is setting up his education policy to benefit different groups: straight whites and conservative Christians. This became quite clear with his appointment of Betsy Devos as Secretary of Education. As Devos holds most things public in disdain, the Administration has signaled its desire to ramp up the federal commitment to voucher programs. Now there is abundant evidence that school choice schemes exacerbate stratification along both socioeconomic and racial lines, among other nefarious effects such as skimming and drafting. These schemes also funnel money away from already strapped public schools and into private schools. So, the clear beneficiary of the national school choice program that the Trump Administration wants to create will be private Christian schools, which draw in the vast majority of students who attend private schools through voucher programs in many states.

Toward this end, the administration has proposed allocating an additional $1.4 billion for school choice programs and eliminating two programs that provide funding for teacher preparation and after-school programs. Overall, Trump's proposed budget for education seeks to cut education spending by 13%, cut student aid programs, and end policies aimed at protecting student loan borrowers. Cutting spending for public schools at the federal level while pumping more money into choice programs has two local effects. First, it forces already financially strapped schools to look elsewhere for funding and this is usual corporate funding with many strings attached. Second, promoting choice programs drains already strapped schools further of much needed cash since school funds follow students. In Chapter 3, I reviewed some studies that noted the financial losses to public schools. Such studies corroborate the conclusion of Moody's Investors Service (2013), hardly a bastion of progressivism, that "Charter schools [and, I would add, other choice schemes] can pull students and revenues away from districts faster than the districts can reduce their costs," creating negative credit pressure on school districts. In the end, if the Trump administration gets its way, what we will see is a huge growth in the role of EMOs generally, and for-profit EMOs specifically. Put simply, this is private theft of a public good, accumulation by dispossession. Under the new Trump corporate order, such accumulation becomes the unquestioned and commonsensical modus operandi. So, clearly, as regards policy, Marxist analyses remain important as capitalist ideology continues to drive policy and shape, therefore, the material conditions within schools.

To counter this, I have suggested the right to the school, which entails applying the right to the publicity of the city to the ways that schools function. "The requirements of justice," Young (2011) argues, "concern less the making of cultural rules than providing institutional means for fostering politicized cultural discussion, and making forums and media available for alternative cultural experiment and play" (p. 152). Toward this end, I have argued that the city must come into the school and the students must go into the city. Further, a principal means of fostering politicized cultural discussion is radical community service learning, which engages Illich's webs in a much more focused way that provides the possibility of shaping autonomy toward the reshaping of the general will. This not only destabilizes the material conditions of schools that tend to reinscribe capitalist social relations but also brings different individuals and groups together in different spaces and contexts to which all can claim to belong.

Even as the autonomous subject is rendered as an individual in traditional liberal theory, there is certainly no inconsistency in engaging a politics of group difference or identity politics. For people are oppressed by their group membership. But, more positively, people become who they are through their group membership. In this vein, Will Kymlicka (1995), for example, stakes out a form of liberal-communitarianism that recognizes the necessity of group protections while rejecting internal restrictions. In other words, oppression at the group level must be challenged and solidarity promoted, but this latter cannot entail restricting individual questioning of the norms and values of the group. Liberation is not the transcendence of group difference, but positive self-definition of such difference (Young, 2011).

Critical Multicultural Education

This discussion now takes us to a somewhat different place, beyond critical pedagogy generally to critical multiculturalism specifically. *Critical* multiculturalism builds on critical pedagogy from its Marxist foundation both as philosophy and method, extending it to the positive recognition of group differences beyond class. Multicultural education has, of course, taken somewhat vulgar forms which function as a form of "managed care" (Garvey, 1996), as noted in the introduction. This has served to placate liberal multiculturalists while fetishizing multiculturalism through Black History Month and "heroes and holidays" approaches. Banks (1988), recall, has described this as "the contributions approach."

Nevertheless, the basic multicultural, the introduction of different cultures, is clearly important to critical *multicultural* education. Here, to see the connection once again with the right to the city, we should contrast fetishizing with eroticism. Eroticism is one of the four virtues of city life discussed by Young (2011), the others being differentiation without exclusion, variety, and publicity. Eroticism, writes Young,

> instantiates difference as the erotic, in the wide sense of attraction to the other, the pleasure and excitement of being drawn out of one's secure routine to encounter the novel, strange and surprising. The erotic dimension of the city has always been an aspect of its fearfulness, for it holds out the possibility that one will lose one's identity, will fall. But we also take pleasure in being open to and interested in people we experience as different. (p. 239)

Fetishization is not about the living encounter that prods the question of our routine. It is about finding the fixed and knowable other; it is necrophilic in its dependence on stasis. *Critical* multiculturalism, then, is about this prodding. It is not only "the process by which an oppressed group comes to define and articulate the social conditions of its oppression," as Young (2011, p. 253) suggests. But also, it is the process through which the dominant group finally understands that "your" cause and "your" oppression are also mine.

This project is not about multicultural education per se and many other authors (Jim Banks, Sonia Nieto, Christine Sleeter, Paul Gorski, etc.) engage that conversation quite well. The thrust of this chapter has been to point out the problem with identity politics. More importantly, it is to suggest that critical multicultural education does not allow multicultural education to settle into siloed identity politics but, instead, works toward a more egalitarian ethos generally, that which, I have suggested, builds from Marx. A politics of difference in education can only create the swerves necessary to the encounter to the extent that it helps create a new dialectic of the political and the cultural. This is best served by educating in the space between the school and society. This is a space opened by a radical right to the city *and* the school.

Notes

1. While Bill Clinton, for example, is seen in the United States as being on the political left, it was his neoliberal pursuit of deregulation that arguably led to the recession under George W. Bush. Clinton signed into law the removal of the firewall between investment banks and commercial banks.

2. Even as there is a focus on theological truth from the right, there was an interesting discursive shift in the election—first as the left has sought "perspective taking"—a component of critical pedagogy—the right used this very effectively (Kellyanne Conway, an advisor to Trump, famously referred to "alternative facts"), forcing the left to ask what happened to truth. The second shift was the patriotic correctness shift as Trump actually challenged American exceptionalism in part because he knows more than the Generals, he claimed. But he challenged it in a hawkish way that was palatable to conservatives generally.
3. Specifically, Trump received the following percentage of the vote from these groups: 56% of weekly churchgoers, 60% of white Catholics, 61% of military personnel, 63% of white men, and 81% of evangelicals.

REFERENCES

Acevedo, M. (2019). The autopsy of quality on-line higher education. *Philosophy and Theory in Higher Education*, 1(2).
Abdulkadiroğlu, A., Che, Y. K., & Yasuda, Y. (2011). Resolving conflicting preferences in school choice: The "boston mechanism" reconsidered. *American Economic Review*, 101(1), 399–410.
Abdulkadiroğlu, A., & Sönmez, T. (2003). School choice: A mechanism design approach. *American economic review*, 93(3), 729–747.
Adorno, T. W. (1973). *Negative dialektik*. New York, NY: Continuum.
Adorno, T. W. (1979). Functionalism today. *Oppositions*, 17, 30–41.
Aliakbari, M., & Faraji, E. (2011). Basic principles of critical pedagogy. In *2nd International Conference on Humanities, Historical and Social Sciences IPEDR*, 17, pp. 78–85. Singapore: IACSIT Press.
Althusser, L. (1971). Ideology and state apparatuses (notes towards an investigation). In L. Althusser, *Lenin and Philosophy and Other Essays*, 171–174. New York, NY: Monthly Review Press.
Althusser, L. (2006). *Philosophy of the encounter: Later writings, 1978–87* (F. Matheron & O. Corpet, Eds., G. M. Goshgarian, Trans.). New York, NY: Verso.
Althusser, L. (2014). *On the reproduction of capitalism: Ideology and ideological state apparatuses*. New York, NY: Verso Books.
Alvarez, Z., Calvete, M., & Sarasa, C. S. (2012). Integrating critical pedagogy theory and practice: Classroom experiences in Argentinean EFL teacher education. *Journal for Educators, Teachers and Trainers*, 3, 61–71.

Anderson, B. (2006). *Imagined communities*. New York, NY: Verso.
Anderson, K. (1995). *Lenin, Hegel, and western Marxism: A critical study*. Champaign, IL: University of Illinois Press.
Anyon, J. (2011). *Marx and education*. New York, NY: Routledge.
Anyon, J. (1980). Social class and the hidden curriculum of work. *Journal of education*, 67–92.
Apple, M. W. (2006). *Educating the "right" way* (2nd ed.). New York, NY: Routledge.
Argys, L. M., Rees, D. I., & Brewer, D. J. (1996). Detracking America's schools: Equity at zero cost?. *Journal of Policy Analysis and Management*, 15(4), 623–645.
Aronowitz, S. (2002). Introduction. In M. J. O'Connell (trans.), *Critical Theory: Selected Essays*. New York, NY: Continuum.
Azar, R. (2015). Neoliberalism, austerity, and authoritarianism. *New Politics*, 59. Retrieved from http://newpol.org/content/neoliberalism-austerity-and-authoritarianism.
Baez, B. (2014). *Technologies of government: Politics and power in the "information age"* Charlotte, NC: Information Age Publishing.
Baker, L. (2012). *A history of school design and its indoor environmental standards, 1900 to today*. Retrieved from http://www.ncef.org/pubs/greenschoolshistory.pdf/.
Baker, L., Dreher, M. J., & Guthrie, J. T. (Eds.). (2000). *Engaging young readers: Promoting achievement and motivation*. New York, NY: The Guilford Press.
Baker, B. D., Sciarra, D. G., & Farrie, D. (2010). *Is school funding fair? A national report*. Retrieved 7/19/2013 from www. schoolfundingfairness. org/National_Report_Card_2012. pdf/.
Banks, J. A. (1988). Approaches to multicultural curriculum reform. *The multicultural leader* 1(2), 37–38.
Banwart, D. (2013). Jerry Falwell, the rise of the Moral Majority, and the 1980 election. *Western Illinois Historical Review*, 5, 133–157.
Beegle, D. M. (2003). Overcoming the silence of generational poverty. *Talking Points*, 15(1), 11–20.
Berlin, I. (1969). *Four essays on liberty*. Oxford: Oxford University Press.
Bertram, C. (2012, Winter Edition). Jean Jacques Rousseau. In E. N. Zalta (Ed.), *The Stanford encyclopedia of philosophy*. Retrieved from http://plato.stanford.edu/archives/win2012/entries/rousseau/.
Bifulco, R., & Reback, R. (2014). Fiscal impacts of charter schools: lessons from New York. *Education Finance and Policy*, 9(1), 86–107.
Boaler, J., Wiliam, D., & Brown, M. (2000). Students' experiences of ability grouping—Disaffection, polarization and the construction of failure. *British Educational Research Journal*, 26, 631–648.
Boekaerts, M., Pintrich, P. R., & Zeidner, M. (Eds.) (2000). Self-regulation: An introductory overview. New York, NY: Academic Press.
Bowles, S., & Gintis, H. (1976). *Schooling in capitalist America*. New York, NY: Basic Books.
Bowles, S., & Gintis, H. (2002a). The inheritance of inequality. *Journal of economic Perspectives*, 16(3), 3–30.
Bowles, S., & Gintis, H. (2002b). Schooling in capitalist America revisited. *Sociology of education* 75(1), 1–18.

Boyd, W. (Trans./Ed.). (1962). *The Emile of Jean Jacques Rousseau*. New York, NY: Teachers College Press.

Boyles, D. (Ed.). (2008). *The corporate assault on youth: Commercialism, exploitation, and the end of innocence*. New York, NY: Peter Lang.

Boxley, S. (2017). *Schooling and value: Marxist essays in education, 2006–2016*. East Sussex: Journal for Critical Education Policy Studies.

Brighouse, H. (2006). *On education*. New York, NY: Routledge.

Burch, P. (2009). *Hidden markets: The new education privatization*. New York, NY: Routledge.

Burris, C. C., Welner, K. G., & Bezoza, J. W. (2009). Universal access to a quality education: Research and recommendations for the elimination of curricular stratification. Boulder, CO: National Education Policy Center. Retrieved May 28, 2013, from http://nepc.colorado.edu/files/Epic-Epru_LB-UnivAcc-FINAL.pdf/.

Chmielewski, A. K. (2014). An international comparison of achievement inequality in within-and between-school tracking systems. *American Journal of Education, 120*(3), 293–324.

Chomsky, N. (2016). Requiem for the American dream. In J. P. Scott, K. Nyks, & P. Hutchison (Producers).

Christensen, L. M., Pendergrass, A., & Whetstone, M. (2016). Global citizenship and the Convention on the Rights of the Child through Transformational Education. In L. Nganga & J. Kambutu (Eds.), *Social justice education, globalization, and teacher education* (pp. 173–184). Charlotte, NC: Information Age Publishing.

Christman, J. (2005). Saving positive freedom. *Political Theory, 33*(1), 79–88.

Cole, A. (2005). What Hegel's master/slave dialectic really means. *Journal of Medieval and Early Modern Studies, 34*(3), 577–610.

Counts, G. (1932). *Dare we build a new social order*. New York, NY: John Day.

Dahlbeck, J. (2017). Education and the free will problem: A Spinozist contribution. *Journal of Philosophy of Education, 51*(4), 725–743.

Dewey, J. (1916). *Essays in experimental logic*. Chicago, IL: University of Chicago Press.

Dodd, S. (2009). *Sandra Dodd's big book of unschooling*. Albuquerque, NM: Sandra Dodd.

Dorn, C. (2011). From "liberal professions" to "lucrative professions": Bowdoin College, Stanford University, and the civic functions of higher education. *Teachers College Record, 113*(7), 1566–1596.

Duncan-Andrade, J., & Morrell, E. (2008). *The art of critical pedagogy*. New York, NY: Peter Lang.

Duquette, D. A. (n.d.). Hegel: Social and political thought. *Internet encyclopedia of philosophy*. Retrieved from https://www.iep.utm.edu/hegelsoc/.

Elley, W. B. (2000). The potential of book floods for raising literacy levels. *International Review of Education, 46*(3–4), 233–255.

Erickson, F. (1975). Gatekeeping and the melting pot: Interaction in counseling encounters. *Harvard Educational Review, 45*(1), 44–70.

Fauziah, H., & Latief, A. (2015). The effect of working in heterogeneous and homogeneous pairs on the students' writing skill. *Arab World English Journal, 6*(2), 174–188.

Fishkin, J. (2014). *Bottlenecks: A new theory of equal opportunity.* New York, NY: Oxford University Press.

Fogelman, K. (1983). Ability grouping in the secondary school. In K. Fogelman (Ed.), *Growing up in Great Britain: Papers from the National Child Development Study.* London: Macmillan.

Foucault, M. (1984). *The Foucault reader.* New York, NY: Pantheon.

Foucault, M. (2003). *The essential Foucault: Selections from the essential works of Foucault, 1954–1984.* New York, NY: New Press.

Freedman, S. W., Delp, V., & Crawford, S. M. (2005). Teaching English in untracked classrooms. *Research in the Teaching of English* 40(1), 62–126.

Freire, P. (1973). *Education for critical consciousness* (Vol. 1). Bloomsbury Publishing.

Freire, P. (1976). *Education, the practice of freedom.* San Francisco, CA: Writers and Readers Publishing Cooperative.

Freire, P. (1985). Rethinking critical pedagogy: A dialogue with Paulo Freire. In *The politics of education: Culture, power and liberation* (pp. 175–199). Westport, CT: Bergin & Garvey Publishers.

Freire, P. (1987). *Education for critical consciousness.* New York, NY: Continuum.

Freire, P. (1989). *Pedagogy of the oppressed.* New York, NY: Continuum.

Freire, P. (2006). *Pedagogía de la autonomía: Saberes necesarios para la práctica educativa.* Mexico City: Siglo XXI Editores.

Fromm, E. (1973). *The anatomy of human destructiveness.* New York, NY: Holt, Rinehart, & Winston.

Garland, C. (2012). "We teach all hearts to break": On the incompatibility of education with schooling at all levels, and the renewed need for a de-schooling of society. *Educational Studies,* 48(1), 30–38.

Garvey, J. (1996) My problem with multi-cultural education. In J. Garvey & N. Ignatiev (Eds.), *Race Traitors.* New York, NY: Routledge.

George, S. (1999, March). A short history of neoliberalism. In *Conference on economic sovereignty in a globalising world,* 24. Retrieved from https://www.tni.org/en/article/short-history-neoliberalism/.

Gibson, R. (2006). Paulo Freire and revolutionary pedagogy for social justice. In E. W. Ross & R. Gibson (Eds.), *Neoliberalism and education reform* (pp. 177–215). Cresskill, NJ: Hampton Press.

Giroux, H. A. (1988). *Teachers as intellectuals: Toward a critical pedagogy of learning.* South Hadley, MA: Bergin Garvey.

Giroux, H. A. (2007). *The university in chains: Confronting the Military-Industrial-Academic complex.* Boulder, CO: Paradigm.

Giroux, H. A. (2014). *Neoliberalism's war on higher education.* Chicago, IL: Haymarket Books.

Giroux, H. A., & Giroux, S. S. (2006). Challenging neoliberalism's new world order: The promise of critical pedagogy. *Cultural Studies? Critical Methodologies,* 6(1), 21–32.

Glantz, (2015). *When titans clashed: How the Red Army stopped Hitler.* Lawrence, KS: University Press of Kansas.

Glass, G. V. (2012, January 28). *The problem with value-added measures.* Retrieved from http://ed2worlds.blogspot.com/2012/01/problem-with-value-added-measures.html/.

Glick, S., & Keller, M. (2016, April 19). Social justice warriors are the reason Donald Trump exists. *Claremont independent*. Retrieved from https://claremontindependent.com/social-justice-warriors-are-the-reason-donald-trump-exists/.

Goodman, J. (2018, July 4). *Trump presses aides on Venezuela invasion*. Retrieved from https://www.yahoo.com/news/us-official-trump-pressed-aides-venezuela-invasion-044213413.html/.

Goodstein, L. (2001, September 15). After the attacks: Finding fault. *The New York Times*. Retrieved from https://www.nytimes.com/2001/09/15/us/after-attacks-finding-fault-falwell-s-finger-pointing-inappropriate-bush-says.html/.

Gouldner, A. W. (1980). *The two Marxisms: Contradictions and anomalies in the development of theory*. London: Palgrave.

Gutmann, A. (1987). *Democratic education*. Princeton: Princeton University Press.

Harvey, D. (2005). *A brief history of neoliberalism*. Oxford: Oxford University Press.

Hattie, J. (2009). *Visible learning: A synthesis of over 800 meta-analyses relating to achievement*. New York, NY: Routledge.

Hegel, G. W. F. (1977). *Phenomenology of spirit* (A. V. Miller, Trans.). Oxford: Oxford University Press.

Herman, E. S., & Chomsky, N. (1988). *Manufacturing consent: The political economy of the mass media*. New York, NY: Pantheon.

Hern, M. (Ed.). (1996). *Deschooling our lives*. Gabriola Island: New Society Publishers.

Herrnstein, R. J. & Murray, C. (1994). *The bell curve: Intelligence and class structure in American life*. New York, NY: Free Press Paperbacks.

Hewitt, R. (2005). Priming the pump: 'Educating' for market democracy. In D. R. Boyles (Ed.), *Schools or markets? Commercialism, privitization, and school-business partnerships* (pp. 47–58). Mahwah, NJ: Laurence Erlbaum.

Heybach, J. A., & Sheffield, E. (2014). Creating citizens in a capitalistic democracy: A struggle for the soul of American citizenship education. In J. E. Petrovic & A. M. Kuntz (Eds.), *Citizenship education around the world: Local contexts and global possibilities*. New York, NY: Routledge.

Hinchey, P. H. (2004). *Becoming a critical educator: Defining a classroom identity, designing a critical pedagogy*. New York, NY: Peter Lang.

Hirsch, E. D. (1996). *The schools we need and why we don't have them*. New York, NY: Doubleday.

Holley, P. (2016, November 2). KKK's official newspaper supports Donald Trump for president. *The Washington Post*. Retrieved from https://www.washingtonpost.com/news/post-politics/wp/2016/11/01/the-kkks-official-newspaper-has-endorsed-donald-trump-for-president/?noredirect=on&utm_term=.95a6b6c58480/.

Holt, J. (1976). *Instead of education: Ways to help people do things better*. New York, NY: E. P. Dutton.

Holt, J. (2016). *Growing without schooling: The complete collection*. Medford, MA: HoltGWS.

Horkheimer, M. (1972). *Critical theory: Selected essays*. New York, NY: Crossroad Publishing.

Horkheimer, M. (1993). The present situation of social philosophy and the tasks of an institute for social research. In *Between philosophy and social science: Selected early writings* (G. F. Hunter, M. S. Kramer & J. Torpey (trans.) (pp. 1–14). Cambridge, MA: MIT Press.

Horton, M., Kohl, J., & Kohl, H. (1990). *The long Haul*. New York, NY: Teachers College Press.
Howe, K. R. (1997). *Understanding equal educational opportunity*. New York, NY: Teachers College Press.
Ignatiev, N., & Garvey, J. (2014). *Race traitor*. New York, NY: Routledge.
Illich, I. (1972). *Deschooling society*. New York, NY: Harper & Row.
Jeffreys, B. (2015, December 21). Rising numbers of pupils home educated. *BBC news*. Retrieved from http://www.bbc.com/news/education-35133119
Jhally, S. (Producer). (2003). *Captive audience*. Northampton: Media Education Foundation.
Kerckhoff, A. C. (1986). Effects of ability grouping in British secondary schools. *American Sociological Review, 51*, 842–858.
Keynes, J. M. (1936). The general theory of money, interest and employment. In E. Johnson & D. Moggridge (Eds.), *The collected writings of John Maynard Keynes, 7*. Cambridge: Cambridge University Press.
Kohn, A. (1999, March). From degrading to de-grading. *High school magazine*.
Kornfeld, J. (2005). Framing the conversation: Social Studies education and the neoconservative agenda. *The Social Studies, 96*(4), 143–148.
Kraut, R. (2018, Summer). Aristotle's ethics. In E. N. Zalta (Ed.), *The Stanford encyclopedia of philosophy*. Retrieved from https://plato.stanford.edu/archives/sum2018/entries/aristotle-ethics/.
Krumboltz, J. D., & Yeh, C. J. (1996). Competitive grading sabotages good teaching. *Phi Delta Kappan, 78*(4), 324–326.
Kuntz, A. M. (2014). Foreword. In B. Baez (Ed.), *Technologies of government in the information age* (pp. vii–xv). Charlotte, NC: Information Age Publishing.
Kuntz, A. M. (2015). *The responsible methodologist: Inquiry, truth-telling, and social justice*. Walnut Creek, CA and New York, NY: Left Coast Press and Routledge.
Kuntz, A. M., Petrovic, J. E., & Ginocchio, L. (2012). A changing sense of place: A case study of academic culture and the built environment. *Higher Education Policy, 25*, 433–451.
Kuntz, A.M., Gildersleeve, R.E., & Pasque, P. (2011). Obama's American Graduation Initiative: Race, Conservative Modernization, and a Logic of Abstraction. *Peabody Journal of Education, 86*, 488–505.
Kuntz, A. M., & Petrovic, J. E. (2018). (Un)fixing education. *Studies in Philosophy and Education, 37*(1), 65–80.
Kymlicka, W. (1995). *Multicultural citizenship*. Oxford: Clarendon Press.
Laclau, E. (1984). The controversy over Materialism. In S. Hänninen & L. Paldón (Eds), *Rethinking Marx* (pp. 39–43). Berlin: Argument.
Landmann, M. (1977). Foreword. In Z. Tarr (Ed.), *The Frankfurt school*. Hoboken, NJ: John Wiley.
Lareau, A. (2003). *Unequal childhoods: Race, class, and family life*. Berkeley, CA: University of California Press.
Lasker, G. A., Mellor, K. E., Mullins, M. L., Nesmith, S. M., & Simcox, N. J. (2017). Social and environmental justice in the chemistry classroom. *Journal of Chemical Education, 94*, 983–987.

Lee, E., Menkart, D., & Okazawa-Rey, M. (2011). *Beyond heroes and holidays.* Washington, DC: Teaching for Change.

Lefebvre, H. (1991). *The production of space* (D. Nicholson-Smith, trans.). Oxford: Blackwell.

Legum, J. (2016). Is Hillary Clinton right about Trump supporters? This is what the polling data says. Retrieved from https://thinkprogress.org/is-hillary-clinton-right-about-trump-supporters-this-is-what-the-polling-data-says-2b37625a1df3/.

Lilla, M. (2016, November 18). The end of identity liberalism. *The New York Times.* Retrieved from https://www.nytimes.com/2016/11/20/opinion/sunday/the-end-of-identity-liberalism.html/.

Locke, J. (1823). *The works of John Locke.* Retrieved from http://oll.libertyfund.org/titles/locke-the-works-of-john-locke-in-nine-volumes/.

Lorde, A. (1984). The master's tools will never dismantle the master's house. In A. Lorde (Ed.), *Sister outsider: Essays and speeches* (pp. 110–114). Berkeley, CA: Crossing Press.

MacSwan, J. (2000). The threshold hypothesis, semilingualism, and other contributions to a deficit view of linguistic minorities. *Hispanic Journal of Behavioral Sciences, 22*(1), 3–45.

Mangubhai, F. (2001). Book floods and comprehensible input floods: Providing ideal conditions for second language acquisition. *International Journal of Educational Research, 35*(2), 147–156.

Mansell, W., & Edwards, P. (2016, April 12). DIY schooling on the rise as more parents opt for home education. *The Guardian.* Retrieved from https://www.theguardian.com/education/2016/apr/12/home-schooling-parents-education-children-england/.

Martin-Jones, M., & Romaine, S. (1986). Semi-lingualism: A half-baked theory of communicative competence. *Applied Linguistics, 7*(1), 26–38.

Marx, K. (1964). *Economic and philosophic manuscripts of 1844* (M. Milligan, trans.). New York, NY: International Publishers.

Marx, K. (1977). *Capital: A critique of political economy* (B. Fowkes, Trans.). New York, NY: Vintage.

Marx, K. (1978). *The Marxist reader.* (R. Tucker, Ed.). New York, NY: Norton.

Marx, K., & Engels, F. (1947). *The German ideology* (R. Pascal, Ed.). New York, NY: International Publishers.

Masciotra, D. (2017, May 7). Stop blaming "identity politics": With white liberals like these, who needs the right wing? *Salon TV.* Retrieved from https://www.salon.com/2017/05/07/stop-blaming-identity-politics-with-liberals-like-these-who-needs-the-right-wing/.

Maybee, J. E. (2016, Winter). Hegel's dialectics. In E. N. Zalta (Ed.), *The Stanford encyclopedia of philosophy.* Retrieved from https://plato.stanford.edu/archives/win2016/entries/hegel-dialectics.

McGinnis, E. I. (Producer). (2011). *Precious knowledge.* Tucson, AZ: Dos Vatos Films.

McLaren, P., & Farahmandpur, R. (2004). *Teaching against global capitalism and the new imperialism: A critical pedagogy.* New York, NY: Rowman & Littlefield Publishers.

McLaren, P. (1989). *Life in Schools.* New York, NY: Longman.

McLaren, P., & Kincheloe, J. L. (Eds.). (2007). *Critical pedagogy: Where are we now?* New York, NY: Peter Lang.

McLaren, P., & Muñoz, J. S. (2000). Contesting whiteness. In P. McLaren & C. Ovando (Eds.), *The politics of multiculturalism and bilingual education: Students and teachers caught in the cross fire* (pp. 22–49). Boston, MA: McGraw-Hill.

McMurrer, J. (2007). *Choices, changes, and challenges: Curriculum and instruction in the NCLB era.* Washington, DC: Center for Education Policy.

Meijnen, G. W., & Guldemond, H. (2002). Grouping in primary schools and reference processes. *Educational research and evaluation, 8*(3), 229–248.

Mill, J. S. (2002). *On liberty; and, utilitarianism.* Mineola, NY: Dover Publications.

Miron, G., & Applegate, B. (2000). *An evaluation of student achievement in Edison Schools opened in 1995 and 1996.* Kalamazoo: The Evaluation Center.

Miron, G., Urschel, J. L., Mathis, W. J., & Tornquist, E. (2010). *Schools without Diversity: Education Management Organizations, Charter Schools, and the Demographic Stratification of the American School System.* Boulder and Tempe: Education and the Public Interest Center & Education Policy Research Unit.

Miron, G., Horvitz, B., & Gulosino, C. (2013). Full-time virtual schools: Enrollment, student characteristics, and performance. In A. Molnar (Ed.), *Virtual Schools in the US* (pp. 22–36). Boulder, CO: National Education Policy Center.

Morrell, A., & Kiersz, A. (2017, December 4). Seeing how the highest and lowest-earners spend their money will make you think differently about 'rich' vs 'poor'. *Business Insider.* Retrieved from https://www.businessinsider.com/how-high-income-and-low-income-americans-spend-their-money-2017-3/

Murphy, P. K., Firetto, C. M., Li, M., Wei, L., Croninger, R. M. V., Greene, J. A., Locczowski, N. G., & Duke, R. F. (2017). Exploring the influence of homogeneous versus heterogeneous grouping on students' text-based discussions and comprehension. *Contemporary Educational Psychology, 51*, 336–355.

Neill, A. S. (1960). *Summerhill: A radical approach to child rearing.* New York, NY: Hart Publishing Company.

Neuman, S. B. (1999). Books make a difference: A study of access to literacy. *Reading Research Quarterly, 34*(3), 286–311.

Neuman, S. B. (2017). The information book flood: Is additional exposure enough to support early literacy development? *Elementary School Journal, 118*(1), 1–27.

Nielsen, K. (1985). *Equality and liberty: A defense of radical egalitarianism.* Totowa, NJ: Rowman & Allanheld.

Nieto, S. (1999). Critical multicultural education and students' perspectives. In S. May (Ed.), *Critical Multiculturalism* (pp. 191–215). London: Falmer.

Nordin, A., & Sundberg, D. (2014). Introduction: The making and governing of knowledge in the education policy field. In A. Nordin & D. Sundberg (Eds.), *Transnational policy flows in European education* (pp. 9–20). Providence, RI: Symposium Books.

Nozick, R. (1974). *State, anarchy, and Utopia.* Malden, MA: Basic Books.

Oakes, J. (2005). *Keeping track: How schools structure inequality* (2nd ed.). New Haven, CT: Yale University Press.

Olssen, M., & Peters, M. A. (2005). Neoliberalism, higher education and the knowledge economy: From the free market to knowledge capitalism. *Journal of Education Policy, 20*(3), 313–345.

Peet, R. (2003). *Unholy trinity: The IMF, World Bank, and WTO*. New York, NY: Zed Books.

Bacon, P. (2017, Sept). Trump hasn't Dismantled Obama's legacy yet—And may not ever. *FiveThirtyEight*. Retrieved from https://fivethirtyeight.com/features/obama-v-trump/.

Petrovic, J. E. (1998). Dewey is a philistine and other grave misreadings. *Oxford Review of Education, 24*(4), 513–520.

Petrovic, J. E. (2001). Educational policy and nationalism: Dewey on balancing cultural and political communities. *Insights, 34*(2), 4–10.

Petrovic, J. E. (2003). Promoting a primary good in schools: An Aristotelian defense of bilingual education. *Philosophy of Education, 2002*, 382–390.

Petrovic, J. E. (2014). *A post-liberal approach to language policy in education*. Bristol: Multilingual Matters.

Petrovic, J. E. (2017). "Review of Boxley, S. (2017). Schooling and Value: Marxist Essays in Education, 2006–2016. Brighton, UK: The Institute for Education Policy Studies." *Policy Futures in Education, 16*(3), 365–367.

Petrovic, J. E. & Kuntz, A.M. (2018). Invasion, Alienation, and Imperialist Nostalgia: Overcoming the Necrophilous Nature of Neoliberal Schools. *Educational Philosophy and Theory, 50*(10), 957–969.

Petrovic, J. E., & Rolstad, K. (2017). Educating for autonomy: Reading Rousseau and Freire toward a philosophy of unschooling. *Policy Futures in Education, 15*(7–8), 817–833.

Petrovic, J. E., & Rosiek, J. (2003). Disrupting the heteronormative subjectivities of Christian pre-service teachers: A Deweyan prolegomenon. *Journal of Equity and Excellence in Education, 36*(2), 161–169.

Pinto, L. E. (2012). *Curriculum reform in Ontario: 'Common sense' policy processes and democratic possibilities*. Toronto: University of Toronto Press.

Platoff, E. (2018, May 24). A gay Texas teacher is on leave after she showed students a photo of her wife. She has few legal protections. *The Texas Tribune*. Retrieved from https://www.texastribune.org/2018/05/24/mansfield-isd-texas-art-teacher-LGBTQ-few-legal-protections/.

Rae, G. (2012). Hegel, alienation, and the phenomenological development of consciousness. *International Journal of Philosophical Studies, 20*(1), 23–42.

Ramstetter, C., & Murray, R. (2017). Time to play: Recognizing the benefits of recess. *American Educator, 41*(1), 17–23.

Rawls, J. (1971). *A theory of justice*. Cambridge, MA: Harvard University Press.

Roberts, P. (2014). Tertiary education and critical citizenship. In J. E. Petrovic & A. M. Kuntz (Eds.), *Citizenship education around the world: Local contexts and global possibilities* (pp. 220–236_). New York, NY: Routledge.

Rolstad, K. (2012). *From Illich and Holt to Papert and Khan: How unschooling became possible and powerful*. Paper presented at the annual meeting of the American Association for the Advancement of Curriculum Studies (AAACS), Vancouver.

Rosaldo, R. (1993). *Culture & truth: The remaking of social analysis*. Boston, MA: Beacon Press.

Ross, E. W. (2015). Broadening the circle of critical pedagogy. In N. E. McCrary & E. W. Ross (Eds.), *Working for social justice inside and outside the classroom* (pp. 209–218). New York, NY: Peter Lang.

Rousseau J. J. (1762a). *Emile, or, on education*. Retrieved from http://www.gutenberg.org/cache/epub/5427/pg5427.html/.

Rousseau, J. J. (1762b). *The social contract or principles of political right*. Retrieved from http://www.constitution.org/jjr/socon.htm/.

Rousseau, J. J. (1964). *The first and second discourses* (R. D. Masters, trans.). New York, NY: St. Martin's Press.

Rowe, B. D. & Klassman, T. L. (2013). An educational dystopia: Mary Shelley's Frankenstein and race to the top. In E. Sheffield & J. Heybach (Eds.), *Dystopia and education: Insights into theory, praxis, and policy in an age of utopia-gone-wrong*. Charlotte, NC: Information Age Publishing.

Rubin, B. C. (2006). Tracking and detracking: Debates, evidence, and best practices for a heterogeneous world. *Theory into practice, 45*(1), 4–14.

Scanlon, T. M., Jr. (1972). Rawls' theory of justice. *University of Pennsylvania Law Review, 121*, 1020.

Schiller, J. (2016). Promoting human rights education in teacher education: A pedagogy for social justice, In L. Nganga & J. Kambutu (Eds.), *Social justice education, globalization, and teacher education* (pp. 185–213). Charlotte, NC: Information Age Publishing.

Shannon, P. (2007). Reading Marxism. In E. W. Ross & R. Gibson (Eds.), *Neoliberalism and education reform* (pp. 161–176). New York, NY: Hampton Press.

Sheffield, E. C. (2011). *Strong community service learning: Philosophical perspectives*. New York, NY: Peter Lang.

Sheffield, E. C. (2015). Toward radicalizing community service learning. *Educational Studies, 51*(1), 45–56.

Shiva, V. (2016). *Water wars: Privatization, pollution, and profit*. North Atlantic Books.

Shor, I. (1992). *Culture wars: School and society in the conservative restoration*. Chicago, IL: University of Chicago Press.

Simons, M., Masschelein, J., & Quaghebeur, K. (2005). The ethos of critical research and the idea of a coming research community. *Educational Philosophy and Theory, 37*(6), 817–832.

Skutnabb-Kangas, T., Phillipson, R., & Rannut, M. (1995). *Linguistic human rights: Overcoming linguistic discrimination*. Berlin/New York, NY: Mouton de Gruyter.

Soja, E. W. (2010). *Seeking spatial justice*. Minneapolis, MN: University of Minnesota Press.

Sotiris, P. (2014). Encounter, inexistence of the origin, and virtual forms of communism: Althuseer's new materialist practice of philosophy in the 1970s. Paper presented at the historical materialism conference, London.

Spring, J. (2017). *American education* (18th ed.). New York, NY: Routledge.

Springer, S., Lopes de Souza, M., & White, R. J. (2016). Introduction: Transgressing frontiers through the radicalization of pedagogy. In S. Springer, M. Lopes de Souza, & R. J. White (Eds.), *The radicalization of pedagogy: Anarchism, geography, and the spirit of revolt* (pp. 1–26). New York, NY: Rowman & Littlefield.

Steger, M. B., & Roy, R. K. (2010). *Neoliberalism: A very short introduction*. Oxford: Oxford University Press.

Stenglein, F., & Mader, S. (2016). Cycling diaries: Moving towards an anarchist field trip pedagogy. In S. Springer, M. Lopes de Souza, & R. J. White (Eds.), *The radicalization of pedagogy: Anarchism, geography, and the spirit of revolt* (pp. 223–246). New York, NY: Rowman & Littlefield.

Stevens, E. (1994). *What is unschooling? The natural child project*. Retrieved from https://www.naturalchild.org/guest/earl_stevens.html/.

Stirk, P. M. (1992). *Max Horkheimer: A new interpretation*. New York, NY: Rowman & Littlefield.

Strober, M. H., & Tyack, D. (1980). Why do women teach and men manage? *Signs, 5*(3), 494–503.

Suchting, W. (2004). Althusser's late thinking about materialism. *Historical Materialism, 12*(1), 3–70.

Symeonidis, V. (2014). Learning the free market: A critical study of neoliberal influences on Sweden's education system. *International Journal of Educational Policies, 8*(1), 25–39.

Tarr, Z. (1977). *The Frankfurt school: The critical theories of Max Horkheimer and Theodor W. Adorno*. New York, NY: John Wiley.

Teachers to your home. (2018, July 27). *Increase in home schooling in the UK*. Retrieved from https://www.teacherstoyourhome.co.uk/articles/significant-increase-in-home-schooling-in-the-uk/.

Thompson, J. B. (1990). *Ideology and modern culture*. Stanford, CA: Stanford University Press.

Toro, F. (2016). Educating for earth consciousness: Ecopedagogy within early anarchist geography. In S. Springer, M. Lopes de Souza, & R. J. White (Eds.), *The radicalization of pedagogy: Anarchism, geography, and the spirit of revolt* (pp. 193–221). New York, NY: Rowman & Littlefield.

Tyack, D. & Cuban, L. (1995). *Tinkering toward utopia*. Cambridge, MA: Harvard University Press.

U.S. Department of Education (2010). *The new normal: Doing more with mess—Secretary Arne Duncan's Remarks at the American Enterprise Institute*. Retrieved from https://www.ed.gov/news/speeches/new-normal-doing-more-less-secretary-arne-duncans-remarks-american-enterprise-institute/.

U.S. Department of Education, National Center for Education Statistics. (2013). *Parent and family involvement in education, from the national household education surveys program of 2012* (NCES 2013-028).

van Dijk, T., & Mensch, C. (2015). *Entrepreneurship education in Swedish compulsory schools: The perception and implementation from an educator's viewpoint*. Lund: Lund University School of Economics and Management.

Van Manen, M. (1990). *Researching lived experiences*. Albany, NY: State University of New York Press.

Vassallo, S. (2013). Critical pedagogy and neoliberalism: Concerns with teaching self-regulated learning. *Studies in Philosophy and Education, 32*, 563–580.

Venkatakrishnan, H., & Wiliam, D. (2003). Tracking and mixed-ability grouping in secondary school mathematics classrooms: A case study. *British Educational Research Journal, 29*(2), 189–204.

Wellmer, A. (2014). On critical theory. *Social Research: An International Quarterly, 81*(3), 705–733.

White, J. (2002). Education, the market and personal well-being. *British Journal of Educational Studies, 50*(4), 442–456.

Will, G. (2006). Ed schools vs education. *Newsweek* 147(3), 98.

Will, M. (2018, March). Teachers Push Back Against Betsy DeVos' Claim That Schools Are in the 'Industrial Era'. *Education Week.* Retrieved from http://blogs.edweek.org/teachers/teaching_now/2018/03/betsy_devos_innovation_industrial.html?cmp=soc-edit-tw/.

Willis, P. (1977). *Learning to labour. How Working Class Kids Get Working Class Jobs.* Farnborough: Saxon House.

Winch, C. (2006). *Education, autonomy and critical thinking.* New York, NY: Routledge.

Wink, J. (2005). *Critical pedagogy: Notes from the real world.* New York, NY: Pearson/Allyn & Bacon.

Wink, J. (2011). *Critical pedagogy: Notes from the real world* (4th ed.). New York, NY: Pearson/Allyn & Bacon.

Yorke, H. (2017, July 7). Number of children home taught doubles in six years amid increased competition for school places. *The telegraph.* Retrieved from https://www.telegraph.co.uk/education/2017/07/07/number-children-home-taught-doubles-six-years-amid-increased/.

Young, I. M. (2011). *Justice and the politics of difference.* Princeton University Press.

Zimmerman, B. J., & Schunk, D. H. (2011). Self-regulated learning and performance. In B. J. Zimmerman and D. H. Schunk (Eds.), *Handbook of self-regulation of learning and performance* (pp. 1–12). New York, NY: Routledge.

INDEX

A

ability grouping 60, 120
accumulation by dispossession (see also primitive accumulation) 18, 70, 71, 148
alienation 7, 36, 37–40, 50, 56, 60, 69, 70, 72–76
Althusser, Louis 9–11, 13, 56, 59–64, 66, 69, 74, 79, 81–86, 92, 93, 98, 103, 105, 110, 111, 114, 124, 127, 133
Arizona 24
assessment (vs testing) 97
authenticity (existential) 82, 83, 135
authoritarian 4, 16, 19, 20, 25, 33, 139
autonomy 7, 9, 13, 16, 25, 27–30, 32, 33, 35, 45, 54–56, 66, 82, 83, 86, 88–91, 98–107, 113–117, 122, 126, 133, 149
   collective 9, 45, 56, 103, 104
   illusion of 9, 54, 55, 82, 86, 113, 126

B

banking education/pedagogy 55, 80, 94
biophilia 77
bureaucratism 78, 79

C

capitalism 6, 11, 16, 17, 19–21, 24–26, 33, 38, 40–43, 46, 47, 50, 56, 65, 74, 78, 79, 84, 85, 87, 105, 130, 135–137
   capitalist exploitation 36, 40, 54
   capitalist ideology 54, 83, 148
   capitalist (social) relations 7, 30, 50, 56, 83, 86, 91, 135, 136, 149
   predatory capitalism 16
charter schools 20, 70, 71, 112, 147, 148
class politics 7, 22, 32, 33, 35, 36, 40, 41, 49, 56, 59, 60, 65, 66, 68, 71, 76, 79, 80, 83, 105, 135, 137–141, 146, 149

classical liberalism 19, 25, 27, 32, 33
Clinton, Hilary 138, 140, 141, 146, 150
commercialism 30–32
commodification 10, 112
　self-commodification 74
commodity/ies 22, 38–42, 46, 48, 49, 57, 75, 76, 94, 100, 115
commodity-form 38
competitive grading 10, 60, 80, 81, 85, 94, 101
conscientization 7, 43, 45, 46, 48, 52, 54, 101–103, 107, 133
conservative modernization 4–11, 15–17, 21, 24, 25, 33, 50, 54, 56, 64, 65, 73
conservativism 4, 5, 8, 15, 19
constructivism/t 54, 87, 90, 91
common core standards 50, 101
credentials, credentialism 74, 77, 99, 100, 115
critical democracy 11, 54, 90, 91, 117
critical education 12, 64
critical geography 110
critical multiculturalism 149, 150
critical pedagogues 1, 10, 26, 46–48, 52, 54, 55, 63, 81, 82, 103, 104, 106, 107, 109, 114, 118, 129–133, 145, 146
critical pedagogy 1, 3, 7–9, 12, 13, 34–37, 40, 41, 43, 47–51, 53, 54, 56, 57, 59–61, 63, 81–83, 85, 86, 90, 93, 101, 103, 105, 107, 109, 110, 113, 114, 116–119, 121, 127, 129, 130, 133, 135, 136, 149, 151
critical schooling 12, 127
critical theory 3, 8, 35, 36, 40–43
cultural invasion 10, 69, 77, 84n4
cultural politics 47

D

decolonization 49
deliberative democracy 4
democratic free school 87–89, 116
deschooling 86, 99, 100, 106, 115, 117, 123, 134

Dewey, John 3, 88, 125, 128
dialectic/al 8–10, 12, 36–40, 45, 50, 52, 55, 60, 62, 92, 105, 109–111, 113, 118, 127, 128, 131, 132, 133, 150
　of possession 37, 38, 40
　socio-spatial dialectic 110, 111, 113, 127, 128, 132
difference principle 26
disequilibrium 127–129, 132

E

egalitarian/ism 26, 36, 137, 150
emancipatory reason 8, 47
Emile 91, 93, 94, 101, 102, 130
educational management organizations (EMOs) 64, 70–72, 112, 148
Enlightenment 92
entrepreneurialism 18, 22
essentialism 119, 137
eudaimon 29

F

fetishization 73–76, 96, 150
　fetishized commodity 39
　fetishizing diversity 119
　fetishizing multiculturalism 149
fixed education 110
fixity 4, 5, 7–9, 11, 12, 16–18, 21, 25, 33, 47, 50, 56, 76, 104, 118, 119, 123, 129, 130, 132
flourishing 2, 4, 7–9, 12, 16, 25, 29–33, 35, 43, 45, 55, 56, 75, 86, 90, 91, 100, 102, 103, 106, 117, 121, 122
Foucault, Michel 11, 23, 104
freedom 1–3, 6, 7, 11, 12, 16, 19, 21, 25–33, 37, 39, 45, 47, 51, 56, 63, 77, 83, 88, 90, 91, 93, 94, 98, 101, 102, 104, 106, 107, 114–117, 122, 123, 130, 133, 143
　effective freedom 31–33
　negative freedom 27, 28, 31, 107, 116, 117, 122

positive freedom 27–29, 31, 47
Freire, Paolo 1, 6, 7, 9, 11, 14, 26, 39, 43–45, 47, 49, 55, 57, 69, 72, 73, 75, 80, 86, 98, 101–104, 114, 133

G

governmentality 8, 24, 96
grading (see competitive grading)

H

Hegel, Georg W. F., 7, 9, 36–40, 45, 50–52
   Hegelian rationalism 50, 51
   Hegel's dialectic 36, 109
hegemony 17, 33, 49, 53, 68, 100, 137, 139
   ideological hegemony 17, 100, 139
heterotopias 11, 12
Hirsch, E. D. 2, 3, 12, 68, 121
homeschooling 87–90, 103, 107, 114, 115, 134
homo economicus 18, 30
Horkheimer, Max 6, 8, 35, 40–43, 45, 56, 57, 83
human capital 20, 46, 47, 49, 73, 75, 100

I

identity politics 135–141, 144, 146, 147, 149, 150
Ideological State Apparatus (ISA) 61–63, 77, 85, 86, 90, 105
ideology 2, 4, 9, 10, 17, 18, 33, 39, 53, 54, 56, 59–64, 66–69, 73–76, 80–83, 86, 92, 93, 98, 103, 116, 117, 119, 120, 130, 137, 143, 144, 148
   as it functions through dissimulation 64, 66, 119
   as it functions through distraction 68, 135
   as it functions through fragmentation 64, 68
   as it functions through legitimation 48, 64–66, 120
   as it functions through reification 60, 64, 68, 73, 75
   as it functions through unification 64, 67, 68
imperialist nostalgia 10, 24, 69, 77, 78, 83
individualism 45, 65, 126, 139
   hyper-individualism 16, 18, 30, 45, 65, 98
integration (vs adaptation) 1, 44, 103, 114, 115, 117, 123
interpellation 6, 76, 10, 13, 62, 73, 74, 95, 114, 133
inter-sectionality 140
Investopedia 10

K

know-how 63, 64, 78, 79, 84, 98, 130

L

labor (power) 19, 25, 37–40, 45, 56, 64, 68–70, 74–77, 79, 101, 138
laissez faire capitalism 19, 25
learning webs 106, 123, 124, 131
liberal-communitarianism 149
liberalism 7, 8, 14, 19, 25, 26, 30, 33, 65, 90, 91, 126, 141
   liberal political theory 26, 32
libertarian 19, 27

M

managerial middle class 16, 23, 80
Marx/ism 7–11, 35–41, 50–52, 56, 57, 59, 60, 69, 79, 81–83, 85, 92, 110, 131, 136 150

Marxist 7, 9–11, 35–37, 40, 42, 49, 54, 56, 57, 60, 61, 83, 105, 130, 135, 136, 138, 146, 148, 149
massification 14, 47, 101, 102
materialism 8, 9, 11, 12, 35–37, 40–42, 48, 50–52, 57, 59, 61, 63, 86, 91, 92, 103–105, 110–113 124, 127, 128
  aleatory 92, 110, 111, 113, 124, 127
  of the encounter 86, 92, 110, 111, 116, 124, 128, 150
moral citizenship 11, 86
multicultural education 9, 119, 136, 149, 150

N

necrophilia (necrophilic) 5, 16, 24, 33, 69, 72, 73, 77, 78, 80, 83, 84, 104, 107, 113, 129, 150
neoconservative(s) 4, 16, 19–22, 24, 33, 69, 80, 139
neoliberal 1, 5, 6, 8, 10–12, 14, 15, 18, 20–25, 30, 31, 33, 34, 46, 47, 49, 53, 61, 64, 66, 69, 70, 72–80, 82, 89, 93–102, 104, 106, 107, 110, 112, 113, 116, 125, 129, 132, 138, 147, 150
  neoliberalism 5, 6, 8, 9, 16–18, 21–23, 25, 33, 35, 45, 47, 64, 65, 69, 77–79, 87, 98, 99, 101, 112, 138, 139

O

oppression 11, 35, 36, 42, 45, 49, 57, 69, 83, 136, 137, 139, 141, 145, 149, 150
  linguistic 57

P

paleo-conservatives 139
patriotic correctness 21, 67, 143, 144, 151
Plato 93
political correctness 8, 140–143, 146

politics of difference 136, 150
precariat 31–33, 40
primitive accumulation 18, 69, 72
privatization 16–18, 23, 70, 71, 112
  of education 74
proletariat 31, 41

R

Reagan, Ronald 19, 68, 139, 140
reification 60, 64, 68, 73, 75
repressive state apparatus 66, 105
responsibilization 66, 95, 104, 126
right to the city 112, 113, 150
right to the school 112, 113, 125, 148
Rousseau, J. J. 11, 12, 86, 87, 91–94, 97, 101–103, 105, 107, 114, 115, 123, 124, 130

S

Sanders, Bernie 138–141, 146
school self-evaluation (SSE) 95
self-commodification 74
self-regulated learning 65, 66, 83, 95, 107, 126
semi-lingualism 57
service learning 113, 118, 124–126, 129, 149
  (strong) community service learning 113, 125, 149
  critical service learning 124
social justice 3, 8, 11, 13, 18, 35, 43, 55, 93, 110, 112, 113, 118, 124, 126, 132, 137, 141, 144
Socrates 29, 52
  socratic dialogue 52
solidarity 19, 56, 68, 127, 132, 138, 140, 149
standardized exams 48, 54, 75, 95, 96, 147
standardized testing 65, 74, 76, 80, 82
standards 2, 10, 17, 20, 22, 24, 46, 48, 50, 66, 68, 74, 75, 81, 94, 96

"standards and accountability" 10, 17, 74, 75, 94, 96
superstructure 9, 40, 56, 59–61, 74, 80–83, 85, 86
surveillance 16, 107
   hyper-surveillance 18, 22, 82
Sweden 20–22, 64, 70

T

technocracy 41, 48, 73, 79, 84, 89, 122
technologism 78, 79
Texas 20, 22, 24, 52, 66, 137
Thatcher, Margaret 19, 21
thingification 73, 78
tracking 66, 74, 81, 118–121, 129
Trump, Donald 34, 138, 140–144, 146–148, 151

U

unschooling 1, 11–13, 34, 69, 85–92, 99–101, 103–106, 109, 110, 113–119, 123–125, 129–131, 133, 134
   in school 13, 89, 116–118, 119, 125, 129–131, 133
utilitarian 26, 64

V

value-added 46, 95

Y

Young Hegelians 51

www.ingramcontent.com/pod-product-compliance
Ingram Content Group UK Ltd.
Pitfield, Milton Keynes, MK11 3LW, UK
UKHW022239230426
12048UKWH00018BA/1358